CASINO TOURNAMENT STRATEGY

STANFORD WONG

Pi Yee Press

CASINO TOURNAMENT STRATEGY

by
Stanford Wong
Pi Yee Press

ISBN 0-935926-18-6

Printed in the United States of America

2 3 4 5 6 7 8 9 10

cover photo: Michael McCall

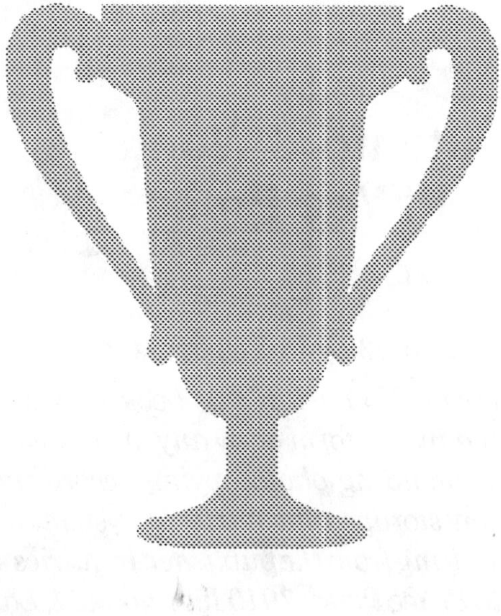

PREFACE

This book includes the complete contents of two predecessors, *Tournament Blackjack* and *Tournament Craps*. Also included are "Tournament Baccarat," "Tournament Keno," and a chapter on matchplay blackjack, three papers previously distributed only to the people who helped develop this tournament material. Much of the other material in this book previously appeared as articles in issues of newsletters that now are hard to find.

In the second printing (1993), the text was made gender-neutral and the cover was improved.

Listed alphabetically are the people to whom I affectionately refer as my teammates. They are among the most skillful tournament blackjack players in the world. They know the material in this book at least as well as I do. They deserve credit for helping develop, refine, and test the ideas in this book. Without them, this material would not be nearly as complete or as easy to learn.

> Ernie Amore
> Anne Amster
> Anthony Curtis
> Dave Douglas
> Blair Rodman

CONTENTS

LIST OF TABLES

CHAPTER 1

INTRODUCTION

Casino games tournaments are fun, and they can be profitable too. Of course a person has to be lucky to win a tournament. This book explains how to win a tournament with less luck than the average person requires.

Tournaments differ from regular casino games in that the contestants compete against each other for the prize money. Whether you win or lose in your bets against the casino does not matter much; what counts is whether you win more (or lose less) than the people you are competing against.

Getting an edge in a casino games tournament means correct money management — betting the right amounts at the right times.

You do not have to have an edge in the game to have an edge in the tournament. Your edge in a tournament comes from being a better tournament player than your opponents.

For prize money you are competing against the other players rather than against the casino. For example, you do not have an edge over the casino in a crap game, but you can get a big edge over the other entrants in a crap tournament. Your edge occurs because most of your opponents have come to play craps and not to play a tournament; they do not use good tournament strategy.

Proper tournament strategy gives you a bigger edge in tournaments in which all contestants bet on the same random outcomes. In a crap tournament, for example, you have a big edge because all contestants bet on the same rolls of the dice. You have a big edge in a baccarat tournament because all contestants bet on the same cards. Likewise you have a big edge in keno tournaments.

You can get an edge in blackjack tournaments, but not as big an edge because each blackjack player gets his or her own cards. This leads to considerable variability, over which you have no control, between the outcomes of your hand and your opponents' hands. If you happen to find a blackjack tournament in which you play the same cards as your opponent, you can get the same big edge that you enjoy in a crap or baccarat tournament.

This book covers getting an edge at tournaments in blackjack, craps, baccarat, and keno. Getting an edge at handicapping tournaments is a chapter in *Betting Cheap Claimers*. Getting an edge in pai gow poker tournaments is a chapter in *Optimal Strategy for Pai Gow Poker* starting with the 1992 edition.

You can get an edge at slot tournaments too, if you have fast fingers. Particularly good are slot tournaments in which you play for a set period of time with your score being the number of credits you rack up, and no cost being assigned for the number of times you push the button to win those credits. In those tournaments, the way to get an edge is to play fast. The faster you can play, the bigger your edge. Play in other than the first session of the tournament so you can watch the early birds and learn how to get the most plays in the allotted time. The machine will not make a mistake, so there is no reason to verify your payoff before playing the next hand. If your neighbor gets a big winner, do not slow down; keep your fingers moving.

Poker tournaments are won by poker skill. Tournament skill has little to do with who wins a poker tournament.

Entry Fees and Prizes

Getting an edge means enjoying a positive expected value. It means if you can play a large number of tournaments you will be a winner overall, though in most individual tournament you will lose.

Part of getting an edge is careful selection of which tournaments to enter. There are differences from tournament to tournament in the relationship of total prize money to total entry fees. Best are tournaments in which total prize money equals or exceeds total entry fees. The casino may also offer free food or free rooms or welcome gifts.

One way to compare total entry fees with total prizes is get a copy of the promised prize structure and add up the numbers. Another is to read the brochure; tournaments giving back 100% or more of the entry fees usually announce it in large type because it is important to prospective entrants.

Tournament pros use the word "equity" to describe the relationship between entry fees and prize money.

When prize money exceeds entry fees, the tournament is said to have "positive equity."

Rules

In any tournament you enter, it is important to familiarize yourself with all the details of all the rules. Any surprises you receive during a tournament due to not knowing a rule will hurt you. For example, sometimes people do not show up for their second-round sessions because they did not realize they qualified.

Generally the rules are printed out. Read them. Even if you already know everything there is to know about playing the game, you cannot know everything about the tournament until you study the details. Pros who have played hundreds of tournaments still read the rules for every tournament they enter. Every big tournament has a rules meeting, generally in a party atmosphere with hors d'oeuvres and refreshments. The party always is fun, but go to the rules meeting anyway even if there is no party. If you have any questions about the rules, ask the tournament director. The only foolish question is the one you do not ask that comes back to bite you in the wallet.

In a tournament you need to know exactly what options are available to the players; they may be different from the rules the casino offers at its real-money tables. How will the round end, and how will you know when the last hand is approaching? Do you get to make a secret bet? How many people from your table will advance to the next round?

Definitions

This book frequently refers to the players according to the relative sizes of their bankrolls. To do this concisely, the following terms are used: BR1 means highest bankroll, BR2 means second-highest bankroll, BR3 means third-highest bankroll, and so forth.

N is the number of people from your table that will advance to the next round of the tournament. BRN means the Nth highest bankroll, which is the smallest bankroll that advances to the next round from this table. If three people advance per table, BRN means BR3.

BR* means any bankroll that advances to the next round. If three people per table advance, then BR* means BR1, BR2, or BR3.

Principles Useful at All (or Most) Casino Tournaments

The following are general principles that underlie the specific strategies presented in the remainder of this book. A good understanding of these principles helps in learning tournament strategies, and also will aid you in developing an appropriate strategy for any tournament situation you might encounter that is not explained in this book.

Succeed or Bust

A large part of your edge comes from applying a simple money-management strategy: Either advance to the next round or bust out trying.

The succeed-or-bust strategy is easiest to understand in tournaments where you know what bankroll total will allow you to advance to the next round. Suppose you buy in with $300 and know for certain that finishing with $600 or more will put you in the next round. You maximize your chance of advancing to the next round by maximizing your chance of turning your initial $300 into $600.

Do not enter a tournament if you cannot afford to lose the whole buy-in. For example, if a tournament requires you to buy in with $1500 and keep what you win (which really means parting with what you lose), then you should not enter that tournament if you are not willing to lose the whole $1500. You have got a big edge over anyone who buys in with $1500 because it is required but is willing to risk only $500 of it, and is not willing to make a bet from the final $1000.

When To Bet Big

You are better off betting small until you know for certain that your present bankroll will not be enough to accomplish your goal. Once you decide that you need to bet big, do it at the first good opportunity, which means picking a spot where if you win you gain on the people you need to catch.

When Behind, Get a Swing; When Ahead, Go With the Flow

If you are behind, try to make a bet that gives you a chance to win while the people you are trying to catch are losing. An obvious example is baccarat; if you are not BR* and everyone with more money than you is betting on bank, you should bet on player. If you are BR*, try to make your bets correlate with those of your most serious competitors so that if they win, you win too.

If Losing a Bet Will Leave You In a Hopeless Position, Bet the Max

Try to avoid getting into the position of having chips left but too few to have a chance. You should have a large enough bankroll to have a chance to advance to the next round, or you should bust out; try to avoid the middle between those two extremes.

For example, suppose only two opportunities to bet remain in the session, you have 180, and the people you are trying to catch have 260 or more. Bet the whole 180. Do not consider betting 90, which is half of your bankroll, because if you lose the 90 your remaining bankroll is helpless against 260. Losing 90 is as bad as losing 180 in that you have no chance to advance either way, but winning 180 can give you a better chance to advance than winning 90.

Flexibility

When you make a big bet, try to make a bet that gives you maximum flexibility. You like to give the casino the smallest percentage possible of course, but if there is a conflict between casino edge and flexibility, go with flexibility.

Give Your Opponent a Chance To Make an Error

If the only way you can win is for an opponent to make a mistake, give that person the opportunity. Just because an opponent can beat you does not mean s/he will beat you.

The Rest of The Book

The rest of this book is divided into four sections: blackjack, craps, baccarat, and keno. Each section gives specific tournament strategy advice.

SECTION A

BLACKJACK

CHAPTER 2
INTRODUCTION
TO TOURNAMENT
BLACKJACK

For blackjack tournaments, tournament skill is considerably more important than blackjack skill. In particular, counting cards is unimportant in a blackjack tournament. Table 1 contains generic basic strategy for blackjack, but learning it is not as important as learning how and when to bet your money. (Technically, basic strategy for blackjack depends on the details of the rules and on how many decks are shuffled together. Table 1 presents a basic strategy that is approximately correct for any set of rules and any number of decks.)

Getting an edge in a blackjack tournament for the most part means correct money management — betting

Table 1
Generic Basic Strategy

Player's Hand				Dealer's Upcard					
	2	3	4	5	6	7	8	9	10	A

double not allowed after split

Player's Hand	2	3	4	5	6	7	8	9	10	A
A-A	spl	spl	spl	spl	spl	spl	spl	spl	spl	spl
10-10	-	-	-	-	-	-	-	-	-	-
9-9	spl	spl	spl	spl	spl	-	spl	spl	-	-
8-8	spl	spl	spl	spl	spl	spl	spl	spl	spl	spl
7-7	spl	spl	spl	spl	spl	spl	h	h	h	h
6-6	h	spl	spl	spl	spl	h	h	h	h	h
5-5	db	db	db	db	db	db	db	db	h	h
4-4	h	h	h	h	h	h	h	h	h	h
3-3	h	h	spl	spl	spl	spl	h	h	h	h
2-2	h	h	spl	spl	spl	spl	h	h	h	h
soft 21	-	-	-	-	-	-	-	-	-	-
soft 20	-	-	-	-	-	-	-	-	-	-
soft 19	-	-	-	-	-	-	-	-	-	-
soft 18	-	dbs	dbs	dbs	dbs	-	-	h	h	h
soft 17	h	db	db	db	db	h	h	h	h	h
soft 16	h	h	db	db	db	h	h	h	h	h
soft 15	h	h	db	db	db	h	h	h	h	h
soft 14	h	h	h	db	db	h	h	h	h	h
soft 13	h	h	h	h	db	h	h	h	h	h
hard 21	-	-	-	-	-	-	-	-	-	-
hard 20	-	-	-	-	-	-	-	-	-	-
hard 19	-	-	-	-	-	-	-	-	-	-
hard 18	-	-	-	-	-	-	-	-	-	-
hard 17	-	-	-	-	-	-	-	-	-	-
hard 16	-	-	-	-	-	h	h	sr	sr	sr
hard 15	-	-	-	-	-	h	h	h	sr	h
hard 14	-	-	-	-	-	h	h	h	h	h
hard 13	-	-	-	-	-	h	h	h	h	h
hard 12	h	h	-	-	-	h	h	h	h	h
11	db	db	db	db	db	db	db	db	db	h
10	db	db	db	db	db	db	db	db	h	h
9	h	db	db	db	db	h	h	h	h	h
8	h	h	h	h	h	h	h	h	h	h
7	h	h	h	h	h	h	h	h	h	h
6	h	h	h	h	h	h	h	h	h	h
5	h	h	h	h	h	h	h	h	h	h

Table 1 Continued

Player's Hand	Dealer's Upcard									
	2	3	4	5	6	7	8	9	10	A
double allowed after split										
A-A	spl	spl	spl	spl	spl	spl	spl	spl	spl	spl
10-10	-	-	-	-	-	-	-	-	-	-
9-9	spl	spl	spl	spl	spl	-	spl	spl	-	-
8-8	spl	spl	spl	spl	spl	spl	spl	spl	spl	spl
7-7	spl	spl	spl	spl	spl	spl	h	h	h	h
6-6	spl	spl	spl	spl	spl	h	h	h	h	h
5-5	db	db	db	db	db	db	db	db	h	h
4-4	h	h	h	spl	spl	h	h	h	h	h
3-3	spl	spl	spl	spl	spl	spl	h	h	h	h
2-2	spl	spl	spl	spl	spl	spl	h	h	h	h

KEY

-:   Stand.

db: Double down; if you cannot double, then hit.

dbs: Double down; if you cannot double, then stand.

h: Hit.

spl: Split.

sr: Surrender; if you cannot surrender, then hit.

Note: Only one pair-split section is needed. If you can double down after splitting, use the pair-split advice on this page. If you cannot double down after splitting, use the pair-split advice on the left.

the right amounts at the right times. It also means proper tournament playing strategy, including playing some hands differently in certain situations from the way you would play them in a regular blackjack game.

This section explains how to play blackjack tournaments. Chapters 2 through 8 were originally published in 1987 as *Tournament Blackjack*. You can learn how to play blackjack tournaments well enough to get an edge. Then you can play them for profit as well as fun.

Let me explain how I wrote this section. Back in December of 1985, I decided to play my first blackjack tournament. I wanted to do well, so I developed my first tournament money-management strategy. I liked my strategy so well that I asked several of my Las Vegas friends if they would be willing to enter the tournament if I paid the entry fee and we shared any prizes won. These friends were not tournament experts at the time; indeed, only one of them had ever played in a blackjack tournament.

After that we played almost every tournament that came along. For each tournament I wrote out ahead of time what I thought would be the best strategies for us to use. My teammates and I learned the strategies and applied them during the tournament. As new situations arose during play, we developed new strategies to handle them. As we discovered better ways to play particular situations, we improved our strategies. Sometimes we made major strategy improvements in the middle of a tournament. After the tournament was over, I rewrote the strategies for that tournament.

Initially we had a different set of strategies for each different tournament format. Gradually relationships between the different strategies emerged, and I was able to combine them into chapters and assemble them into a book.

Thus the material in this book has already been learned and tournament-tested by several people. It may not be perfect, but it gives us a big edge in tournaments.

Some of the ideas in this book are my own, developed either with the aid of a computer or from playing tournaments and then figuring out what happened in a particular situation and why. Some things I learned from watching other players in action. Much of what I know about winning at tournaments I have learned from others. My teammates in particular have contributed many ideas to this book.

We still play tournaments, and before each tournament we sit down and study the chapters that apply to the tournament we are about to play. I study this material myself before each tournament, partially because there is so much to know and partially because tournaments differ from one another so much that different strategies apply to different tournaments.

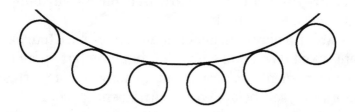

CHAPTER 3
COMPETING
AGAINST PLAYERS
AT ALL TABLES

This chapter applies to the situation where you are competing against more than just the players at your table; you are trying to finish with a higher bankroll than players at a number of tables.

The strategy is to pick out a goal bankroll size that will win. Then go all out for that number or zero. Either bust out or hit your goal.

Succeed or Bust

A large part of your edge comes from applying a simple money-management strategy: Either advance to the next round or bust out.

The succeed-or-bust strategy is easiest to understand in tournaments where you know what bankroll total will allow you to advance to the next round. For example, at one tournament contestants buy in with $500 and know for certain that finishing with $1000 or more will put them in the second round. You maximize your chance of advancing to the second round by maximizing your chance of turning your initial $500 into $1000.

Your average ending bankroll is about the same no matter how you bet your money, and is equal to your beginning bankroll less the casino edge on the bets you make. It also is equal to your probability of finishing with more than $1000 times the average bankroll you end up with if you finish with more than $1000, plus your probability of finishing with less than $1000 times the average bankroll you end up with if you finish with less than $1000. Maximizing your probability of finishing with more than $1000 means stopping as close to $1000 as you can when you make it, and going bust if you do not finish with at least $1000. If you do that, you have almost a 50% chance of turning your initial $500 into $1000 or more.

Setting Your Goal

There seems to be a simple square-root relationship between the proportion of contestants moving on to the next round and the bankroll required to be one of those lucky ones. For example, if one fourth of the contestants are going to advance from round 1 to round 2 of the tournament, a good estimate of the bankroll required is double the starting bankroll. The ratio of entrants to number moving on is 4, and the square root of 4 is 2. When playing in such a tournament, try to double your starting bankroll or bust out.

This relationship holds best for large numbers of contestants advancing to the next round; when twenty or fewer contestants advance, the square-root relationship breaks down.

By being among the last to register for the tournament, you probably can get in the final playing session. This allows you to monitor the earlier sessions to set a better target.

As more and more players learn to go for bust or advance to the next round, the cutoff score will be higher.

Probability of Attaining Your Goal

A good approximation of your probability of achieving any particular target bankroll is the ratio of your present bankroll to your target. Think of it as conservation of expected value. Suppose you need to triple your present bankroll. What is your probability of doing it? Answer: approximately 1/3. Suppose you need to multiply your present bankroll by ten. What is your probability of doing it? Answer: approximately 1/10.

Attaining Your Goal

Try to avoid getting stuck with chips you cannot bet. If you cannot bet a $2.50 chip and the minimum bet is $10, avoid making a bet of $15 or any other odd number unless you are going all in. When the minimum bet is $5 and you cannot bet a $2.50 chip, bet $5 anyway and do not worry if you get a chip you cannot bet.

If Your Goal Is Within One Max Bet Of Your Bankroll

Start out betting a proportion of your bankroll equal to your advantage. Most of the time this means betting the minimum. If you are counting cards and the count is so high (or the rules so liberal) that you have a 2% edge, then bet 2% of your bankroll or less. You might be able to drift into your goal without having to make a big bet. This happens frequently at tournaments where 50% of the field advances to the next round.

If Your Goal Is One To Two Max Bets Above Your Bankroll

You will not be able to drift up to your goal with minimum bets. So if you can count cards, bet the minimum on negative or zero counts and make a large bet on positive counts. If you do not count cards, then bet aggressively whenever you feel like it. You are going to have to make some big bets sometime.

If Your Goal Is More Than Two Max Bets Above Your Bankroll

If your goal is many maximum bets above your current bankroll, then bet aggressively from the first hand. For example, in a winner-take-all tournament with a $100 buy-in and $100 max bets, it is best to go with max bets starting on the first hand.

If your bankroll is greater than the maximum bet but less than double the maximum bet, then bet half your bankroll. For example, if you are trying to turn $600 into $9000 and the maximum bet is $500, start out with a bet of $300.

Last Five Hands

To be able to advance despite finishing up with a string of losses, you would like to be a minimum bet above your goal with a hand to go, two minimum bets above your goal with two hands to go, etc. For example, if you want to finish with at least $600 and the minimum bet is $10, you can smile if you have $650 with five hands to go. But if you have $620 with five hands to go, you are out if you lose all of the last five hands.

In the example of $620 with five hands to go, you can use a progression and finish with $600 or more if you win any one of the last five hands, even if you lose the other four. Bet $20 on the fifth-last hand; if you win, switch to $10 bets and if you lose, you have $600 with four hands to go. If you have $600 with four hands to go, bet $30 on the fourth-last hand; if you win, switch to $10 bets and if you lose, you are down to $570 with three hands to go. Then bet $50; if you win, switch to $10 bets and if you lose, you are down to $520 with two hands to go. Then bet $90; if you win, switch to $10 bets and if you lose, you are down to $430 with one hand to go. A bet of at least $170 on the final hand gives you your last chance to get to $600.

If you win any one of those last five hands, drop to $10 bets the rest of the way and finish with at least $600. Do not double down or split a pair if losing a doubled bet would leave you short of your goal.

On the final hand of a tournament in which a fixed percentage (example: 50%) of the field advances to the next round, bet either the minimum or make a big bet. If you think your score minus a minimum bet will qualify you for the next round, bet the minimum. If you think your score might be short, you might as well bet big and qualify for sure if you win your bet. Do not try to fine-tune it to the point where a slight error in judgment makes you a high-scoring non-qualifier.

Winner-Take-All Tournaments

In some tournaments involving hundreds of contestants, the prize structure rewards the single highest bankroll so highly that you should try only to have that highest bankroll. Register late so as to get into the final session, and find out what the earlier session winners achieved so you can set your goal precisely. Some tournaments have required turning $600 into $6000 or more.

To have a chance in such a tournament, you must bet big virtually all the time. Bet small only if you have reached your goal for the round.

With a maximum bet that is small in relation to your goal, you may not get a big enough random fluctuation to reach your goal. For example, starting with $600 at a game with no house edge and playing until you have zero or $10,000, you have a 6% chance of reaching $10,000. But with play limited to 100 hands and with a $500 maximum bet, you have a 3.4% chance of reaching $10,000 and a 5.1% chance of having some cash left but less than $10,000.

On marginal doubles, double down. On marginal hit/stand, such as sixteen against 10, stand. If you are counting cards, split 10-10 at an index number one less than usual, which yields more splits of 10-10. These plays increase your variance, and thus increase your chance of reaching your goal.

CHAPTER 4
BLACKJACK:
TABLE WINNER
FORMAT

This chapter applies to blackjack tournaments in which you are competing only with the other players at your table. As mentioned in chaper 1, BR* means any bankroll position that advances to the next round, and BRN means the minimum bankroll position that advances to the next round. For example, if the top three winners per table advance to the next round, then BRN means BR3, and BR* means BR1, BR2, or BR3.

Here is a winning tournament strategy: Bet the max on the last hand. Don't laugh; that is a powerful strategy. Later chapters will modify it to make it even more powerful.

This chapter discusses attaining a bankroll position such that winning a max bet on the last hand is sufficient to make you BR*. The best way to do it is by being BR* going into the last hand or busting out trying. The reason is BR*'s probability of winning the table is greater than it should be for the number of chips BR* has, and everyone else's chances are less than they should be.

For example, suppose only one person will advance in the tournament out of three players with bankrolls of 500, 600, and 800. If the game would continue indefinitely, the three players would have probabilities of winning proportional to their bankrolls, i.e. 5/19, 6/19, and 8/19. With just one hand to go, however, the probabilities are .1, .2, and .7. BR2 and BR3 are not getting full value for their chips. Their chances of winning the table would have been better had they bet more aggressively earlier, either taking over the BR1 spot or busting out.

Money-Management Strategies

Here are the four money-management strategies to be used at various times. The rest of this chapter explains exactly when to use each strategy.

Proportional Betting

Bet a proportion of your bankroll equal to or slightly less than your edge over the dealer. (Since the variance of outcomes for one blackjack hand is around 1.2, you actually should bet only about 80% of your edge.) If you are not counting cards, this means betting the minimum. If you are counting cards, you will find that seldom will your edge get high enough to justify betting more than the minimum.

Bet With the Flow

Whatever your opponents are betting, you bet. If they all bet around 100, bet 100.

Bet Contrary

Whatever your opponents are betting, bet the opposite. If they bet small, bet big. If they bet big, bet small.

Progression

To give yourself as many chances of hitting your target as possible, use a progression. This means betting either 1/7, 1/3, or all of your bankroll. If you bet 1/7 and lose, then bet 1/3. If you lose a bet of 1/3 of your bankroll, then bet the remainder of your bankroll. All you have to do is win one bet to hit your target. (Theoretically you could bet 1/15 also, but as a practical matter you probably will never have an opportunity to bet that fraction.)

If you cannot bet that precise amount, round down. When betting a progression, do not double, do not split, and do not buy insurance.

The reason for these precise fractions is that if you lose, you can bet the next-higher fraction, which amounts to approximately doubling your bet. All you have to do is win one bet to bring your bankroll up to where you want it to be.

Table 2 has the probabilities of success for each fraction of your bankroll with which you start a progression.

For example, suppose you start with 840 and bet 1/7 of it or 120, and if you lose it your next bet is 240, and if you lose that you bet your last 480. If you win any one of those bets, your bankroll is 960. You have an 86% chance of turning 840 into 960, and a 14% chance of turning 840 into zero.

Table 2
Probability of Success for a Progression

fraction	prob. of success
1/7	.86
1/3	.73
1	.48

Betting on the Early Hands

Start with proportional betting. Until the last ten hands or ten minutes, as long as you are BR* or close to it, stick with proportional betting.

If You Fall Significantly Behind

Sometimes you will fall behind BRN by quite a bit. If the people ahead of you are betting wildly, continue to use proportional betting and wait for them to lose their chips.

If the people ahead of you are betting so small that you do not think you can catch them with proportional betting, then use a progression. Which fraction of your bankroll you select depends on how much money you need to win to be BR*. Select either 1/7, 1/3, or all of your bankroll, and if you have to round then round down.

Here is an example. About half-way through the match at the final table of a blackjack tournament, my bankroll was the lowest out of all six players; I had $420. The leader had $530, and he was betting $5 per hand. I wanted to be BR1. 1/7 of my bankroll was $60, but winning $60 would not make me BR1. 1/3 of my bankroll was $140, and winning $140 would make me BR1. So I bet $140. If that bet lost, my intention was to bet my remaining $280. Winning either of the two bets would make me BR1. With no doubling and no splitting, I had a 73% chance of becoming BR1 and a 27% chance of busting out.

The time to switch from proportional betting to a progression is when you know you cannot get a BR* spot with proportional betting, and when betting 1/7 or 1/3 of your bankroll will give you the position you want without too much to spare. If you are in doubt as to whether to use a progression or stick with proportional betting, stick with proportional betting until five or ten hands from the end.

In the above example, I considered switching to a progression earlier when I could have taken over the BR1 spot by winning an amount equal to 1/7 of my bankroll, but the count was negative so I decided to wait. While I was waiting, I dropped farther behind BR1, and winning an amount equal to 1/7 of my bankroll no longer was enough to catch him. I made my move when I did for two reasons. First, the count was high. Second, winning an amount equal to 1/3 of my bankroll would give me the lead, but not by much. If I had held off for a few more hands, my bankroll might have shrunk to the point where winning a bet of 1/3 of it would not have given me the BR1 spot.

When betting a progression, be rigid about the fraction of the bankroll you bet, but not rigid about the rest of the details. For example, if you bet 1/7 of your bankroll on say the fifth-last hand, do not double down because you could not afford to lose the extra money. But if you bet 1/7 of your money earlier than that and get a double-down hand, go ahead and double down because you still have a chance in the tournament even if you lose the doubled bet. Another example: Once you start a progression, do not feel any compulsion to keep it going on the very next hand. Suppose you have 570, bet 1/7 of it or 80, and lose. You can bet 1/3 of your remaining bankroll on the very next hand, or you can hold off for a few hands.

The more good tournament players at your table, and the fewer advancing to the next round per table, the more likely you are to have to use a progression.

If your opponents are betting more than the minimum, you have to reconsider every bet. For example, if you lose a bet of 1/7 of your bankroll and then discover that a bet of 1/3 of your remaining bankroll will not give you the BR* spot even if it wins, then do not bet 1/3 of your remaining bankroll. In other words, bet 1/3 of your bankroll only if winning the bet will make you BR*; do not bet 1/3 just because you have lost a bet of 1/7.

If you cannot catch BR* in one bet due to the maximum being low in relation to your bankroll, then bet contrary to the bets of the people you are trying to catch. For example, in a one-winner tournament with a maximum bet of 100, BR1 was almost 300 ahead of me and bet 100. So I bet the minimum, 5. Had BR1 bet 5, I would have bet 100.

Betting with Ten Hands to Go

This is the time to look around the table and figure out if you are BR*, or what you have to do to become BR*.

If You Are BR*

If you are BR* with ten hands or ten minutes to go, bet with the flow. Whatever the people who are trying to catch you are betting, you should approximately match.

If you are BR* and bet first, make it difficult for your opponents to bet contrary to you. Bet an amount just slightly smaller than your lead. If the maximum bet is small in relation to your bankroll and you bet first, bet half the maximum.

If You Are Not BR*

If you are not BR* with ten hands or ten minutes to go, bet in a manner that gives you a chance to become BR*. If a progression is possible, use it.

If you are farther behind than the maximum bet, bet either the minimum or the maximum, whichever is contrary to BR*. If you have to bet first and thus do not know whether the minimum or the maximum will be contrary to BR*, bet the maximum. If in doubt about whether to bet the minimum or the maximum, bet the max.

Suppose the person you are trying to catch has bet the max. You have a choice between betting the max and hoping to win while your opponent loses, or betting small and hoping your opponent loses. The latter happens 48% of the time, while the former happens only 12% of the time. This is why the best play is to bet contrary. But if you are so far behind that betting contrary cannot close the gap, then bet the max and hope that you win while BR* loses. That is a low-probability route, but if it is your only chance you should take it.

Using a progression is better than betting contrary if you have a choice. Five to ten hands from the end is a good time to start a progression. You want your progression to end before the last hand, because if it ends on the last hand your opponents will make big bets along with you and thus put you on the wrong end of a W-W, L-L decision; that is, you will find yourself in the situation where if everyone wins their big bets, you lose the match, and if everyone loses their big bets, you lose the match. Your chances of winning the match are not very good if you must win your bet while an opponent loses.

And you might get a push, which suggests starting a progression earlier yet.

The last possible hand to start a progression by betting 1/3 of your bankroll is the third-last hand. But if you wait that long, you cannot handle a push. So if you know you are going to have to bet 1/3 of your bankroll sometime, it is best to do it on the fourth-last hand or earlier, so as to be able to handle a push.

The last possible hand to bet 1/7 of your bankroll is the fourth-last hand, and that is really too late because it does not leave room for a push. If you think you can get the BR* spot by betting 1/7 of your bankroll, do it on the fifth-last hand or earlier.

Another reason to start a progression earlier is you are more likely to catch your opponents with minimum bets out. A progression is more effective if you know exactly what you need to beat.

You may make a bet to position yourself for a progression. For example, suppose you have 250, BR* is sitting on 380, and you have at least five hands yet to play. You cannot take the BR* position for yourself by betting 1/3 of your bankroll, which suggests betting your whole bankroll. But betting all 250 at once gives you only a .48 chance of becoming BR*. You can increase your probability of becoming BR* to .60 by betting 50. If you win, you have 300 and your next bet is 1/3 of your bankroll. If you lose the 50, your bankroll is 200 and your next bet is the whole thing. Better to have a .60 chance of becoming BR* with 400 than a .48 chance of becoming BR* with 500.

When you bet 1/7 or 1/3 of your bankroll, do the arithmetic in your head. If you have got a bankroll of 420, you know that a third of it is 140; you do not have to separate your chips into three equal piles to figure it out. You do not want to let your competition know that you are betting any special fraction of your bankroll, lest you inadvertently teach them to become better tournament players.

Of course, as soon as you become BR*, bet with the flow.

Last Five Hands and You Are Not BR*

If in the last five hands you are not BR*, generally it will be for either of two reasons. If you are not BR* because your opponent or opponents have a big lead over you and the max bet is small in relation to your bankroll, you already should be making max bets hand after hand. Keep doing it, and in addition double down more frequently hoping to get a lucky break.

If you are not BR* in the last five hands because an opponent has just moved ahead of you, immediately bet contrary by enough to have a chance to retake the BR* position.

If an opponent wins a large bet and as a result you find that you no longer are BR* and must make a large catch-up bet, then bet either 1/7 or 1/3 or all of your

bankroll, whichever will allow you to regain the BR*
spot. Never bet 1/2 of your bankroll as a catch-up bet,
because losing it would leave you in a virtually hopeless
position; if betting 1/3 of your bankroll will do the job,
then bet 1/3; and if 1/3 would not do the job, then bet the
max (or the minimum, if it is contrary to your opponent's
bet).

Betting on the Next-to-Last Hand

You Are BR*

If you are BR* on the next-to-last hand, your bet
size depends on your lead. If you are ahead by more than
what your most serious competitor can bet, then bet the
minimum. If you are ahead by less than what your most
serious competitor can bet, hold a chip more than that
person has and bet the balance of your bankroll.

You Are Not BR*

If you are not BR* going into the next-to-last hand,
bet big enough to try to be BR*, with one exception. The
exception is that you can settle for being one position
worse than BRN on the last hand if two conditions hold.
The conditions are that you must bet after BR* on the last
hand, and you must be within half a bet of that BR*.

Half a bet means half of the maximum you can bet.
If you have more chips than the maximum bet allowed,
then half a bet is half of the maximum bet allowed. If you
have fewer chips than the maximum bet allowed, then
half a bet is half of your bankroll.

For example, suppose it is time to make a bet on the
next-to-last hand, your table will have one winner, and
you have 450. If you will be betting after BR1 on the last
hand, and you are BR2, and BR1 has less than 675, then
bet the minimum on the next-to-last hand. If you will

have to bet ahead of BR1 on the last hand, bet the max on the next-to-last hand. If your 450 makes you BR3 or worse, bet the max on the next-to-last hand. If BR1 has 675 or more, bet the max on the next-to-last hand (because you are more than half a bet behind).

The reason for the exception is if you are BR2 and within half a bet of BR1, no matter what BR1 bets on the last hand you will have a good chance to win the table, and that chance is better with a big bet on the last hand than a big bet on the second-last hand. Commonly, BR1 will bet small on the last hand, and you can win the table if you win a max bet. Winning the table with a last-hand max bet means your probability of winning the table is .44. If you go up with your max bet on the second-last hand, your probability of winning that hand will be the same .44, but it will not assure you of winning the table because your opponent might pass you on the last hand. A .44 probability of winning is superior to a .44 chance of maybe winning, maybe losing.

If you make a big bet on the second-last hand in an attempt to be BR* for the last hand, play as if a push is as bad as a loss. (See chapter 8 for the appropriate strategy.)

Focus on BR*

The advice to bet 1/3 of your bankroll is not completely rigid for the second-last hand. The important thing is to give yourself a chance to win the table if you win the bet, and still have a chance to win the table if you lose that bet. Betting 1/3 of your bankroll does this automatically. But other numbers might also do. For example, suppose you have 800 and BR* has 840 and now you must bet on the second-last hand. You could bet 280, because that is 1/3 of your bankroll. But any bet between 50 and 370 would give you a chance to become

BR* if you win it, and still leave you a chance to win on the last hand.

The next few chapters explain what you should bet on the final hand.

CHAPTER 5
BLACKJACK:
FINAL HAND, ONE
WINNER PER TABLE

This chapter applies to any situation where there is only one winner per table. Use it when only one person advances to the next round, when two people advance but one is so far ahead as to have the lead position locked up, and when several people at the table will receive cash prizes but the prize for the winner is considerably more than the prize for finishing second.

The material in chapter 4 applies for the hands leading up to the final one. By the time you make a bet on the final hand, you should be BR1. Either that or you should have busted out.

BR1 on the Final Hand

Generally you should bet big. The reason is generally there are several competitors who can catch you if they win their final bets, and your probability of winning the table is higher if you bet big yourself rather than if you bet small and hope that all of your competitors lose.

The Two-Player Exception

If you are BR1, you bet first, you have a slim lead over BR2, and BR3 is out of it, bet small. In other words, if you have only one competitor, you are better off trying to win the table by that competitor losing rather than by winning your own bet. If you bet small, you have a 56% chance of winning the table because your opponent has a 44% chance of winning a bet. If you bet big, you have only a 52% chance of winning the table because you have a 48% chance of losing your bet.

Your best bet, if you bet first in a two-person game, is to bet just less than your lead over BR2. For example, if you are ahead by 800 to 500 with a 500 max bet, bet 295. This is superior to betting the absolute minimum for two reasons. First, it automatically covers you in the event both BR2 and you win your bets if it is possible for you to cover that situation. (You like to put BR2 in the position where the only way that person can win the table is to win the hand while you lose yours.) Second is that it gives you the opportunity to beat BR2 by doubling down if that is the only way you have a chance. In this example of 800 to 500, a max-bet natural will bring BR2 up to 1250. If you have bet 295, you can double down no matter what you get (see chapter 8) or double for less (160 will do it) to have a chance to beat 1250. Had you bet 5, you would not have a chance to beat a big-bet natural by BR2.

Win Both Ways

If BR2 bets ahead of you, you should approximately match BR2's bet. You like to be in the position where if both hands win you win the table, and if both hands lose you win the table.

Even better than exactly matching BR2's bet is to keep what BR2 keeps plus a chip. For example, if you lead 800 to 600 and BR2 bets 300, bet 495. BR2 keeps 300 unbet, and you keep 305 unbet. That bet does everything that matching BR2's bet would do in the event both hands lose. It also allows you to win without doubling down in the event BR2 doubles down, which is better than the situation you would be in if you had just matched BR2's bet.

Shut BR2 Out

If your lead is so large that BR2 cannot catch you even with a double down, bet the minimum. Why jeopardize a lock? (If anyone can double down to get ahead of you, you do not have a lock. But if the only way someone can beat you is by getting a natural, then bet as if you have a lock.)

If the only way BR2 can catch you is with a double down, then you are better off betting big. You are close to a .9 favorite if you bet big enough to win the table both ways even if BR2 doubles down, but you are no more than a .7 favorite if you bet so small that you can lose the table to BR2 doubling down. In other words, you should risk BR2 winning the table by winning while you lose, in order to win the table yourself when BR2 doubles down and both hands win.

Shutting out BR3 also has value. You should like to bet less than your lead over BR3. You should also like to bet so small that doubling BR3's bankroll will not catch you.

Selecting a Bet

Sometimes there is a conflict between two things you would like to do. For example, beating BR2 both ways might require a big bet, while shutting out BR3 requires a small bet. If you cannot do both simultaneously you have to make a choice.

When you are first to bet, how likely you are to win the table for a given bet size depends on what your opponents bet after you. Therefore, which bet you select sometimes depends on the skill of your opponents. There are situations you should play one way against a tournament expert and another way against someone who is only guessing as to the best way to bet the hand.

Selection of bet size is explained in the following examples. They examine almost every betting situation you can face as BR1. The expectations have been derived by computer simulation, and are accurate to within 1%. For all close decisions, the accuracy is high enough so that the difference between the choices is statistically significant.

For all of the example, the minimum bet is $5 and the max is $500.

First base is the hand on the right, and third base is the hand on the left. The person to bet first (and play the hand first) is denoted by the puck ❂. Betting proceeds from the puck to third base, and then from first base toward the puck. For those opponents who bet before you, their bets are shown in the circles. Amounts unbet, and total bankrolls of opponents who have yet to make a bet, are shown below the circles. A question mark in a circle indicates the bet the example is asking you to make.

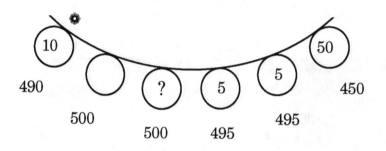

EXAMPLE 1

One Winner
Min 5
Max 500

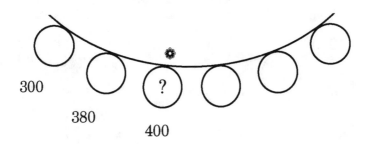

300

380

400

You are BR1, you bet first, two or more other people are close behind you, and your opponents can go all in. Bet the max. In this example a bet of 365 is as effective as a max bet, but a good general rule is to bet the max to automatically cover opponents' naturals as well as they can be covered. Therefore, as BR1 in a crowd, when your opponents can go all in, you should bet the max. Whether you bet first or last or in the middle does not matter; you should bet the max. Your probability of winning the table is at least .44.

You might wonder about the value of betting less than the max if you bet last and can cover the bets of all your opponents with less than a max bet. In other words, should you figure out what is the best any of your opponents could do if they all win their bets, and then bet enough to beat that amount? The answer is yes, but only if you can cover double downs by all opponents. If you cover only single-bet wins by all your opponents and leave yourself open to getting beaten by a double down even if you win your own hand, your probability of winning the table is at most .37, and it can be chopped below .30 if your opponents double down more often than basic strategy suggests.

EXAMPLE 2

One Winner
Min 5
Max 500

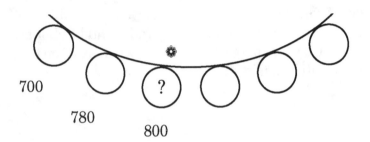

700

780

800

This example differs from the previous one in that BR2 cannot bet all of the bankroll. As in the previous example, you are BR1, you bet first, and two or more other people are close behind you.

If neither of your opponents is a tournament expert, bet the max. Your probability of winning the table is at least .44.

If one of the people with a shot at you is a tournament expert, bet the minimum. With two opponents in range, your probability of winning is .42, and the more opponents within range the lower your probability of winning.

If you bet the max, and BR2 bets 390 and doubles down if it is to BR2's advantage to do so (a strategy explained in chapter 8 under the name "Curt's Revenge"), your probability of winning the table is only .30.

EXAMPLE 3

One Winner
Min 5
Max 500

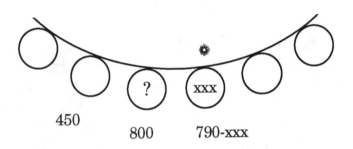

450

800

790-xxx

BR2 is close behind you, and BR3 is far back but still within range.

The example shows you betting after BR2. This is the only time, with these bankrolls, that you consider betting less than the max.

You would like to bet at least 105 to cover the possibility of BR3 doubling the bankroll. You would like to bet no more than 345 to cover the possibility of BR3 betting small and winning the table if you all lose. (Do not worry about that if BR2 has already bet small enough to shut out a push by BR3; one person shutting out BR3 is enough.)

You would also like to match the bet of BR2. If BR2 bets ahead of you and you can approximately match

BR2's bet with a bet between 105 and 345, do it. For example, if BR2 bets 200 and you bet second, match the 200 (or keep what BR2 keeps plus a chip, betting 205) for a .64 probability of winning. (If BR2 is a tournament expert who uses Curt's Revenge, your probability of winning by matching the 200 bet is .54. If instead of 200 you bet 400, your probability of winning is .50.)

If the example were changed so that you had to bet first, you should bet the max. If the example were changed so that BR3 leads off with a max bet and you bet second, you should bet the max.

If BR2 bets above 350 and you bet second, there is a conflict between two things you would like to do. You cannot match BR2's bet without betting more than your lead over BR3. You are better off matching BR2's big bet. If BR2 is not a tournament expert, your probability of winning the table is .53; if BR2 is a tournament expert who uses Curt's Revenge, your probability of winning the table is .44. Betting 105 would give you a probability of winning of only .44 regardless of the expertise of BR2.

You also have a conflict if BR2 bets less than 105 and you bet second. For example, suppose BR2 bets 20. If you match it you take a chance that BR3 will double the bankroll to beat you. In this case you are better off betting the max for a probability of winning of .47. Note that the 345 number does not matter anymore because if you lose your bet BR2 beats you, so you do not care whether BR3 also beats you. If you bet 105 instead of the max, your probability of winning is only .45 because you no longer beat a max-bet natural by BR3. If you match BR2's bet with a bet of 20, your probability of winning is .42 if BR2 is not a tournament expert, and less if BR2 uses Curt's Revenge.

EXAMPLE 4

One Winner
Min 5
Max 500

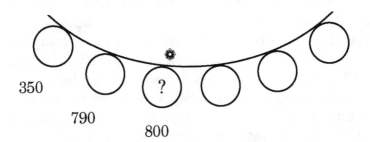

350

790

800

This example differs from the previous one in that now BR3 is out of it if you bet 95 or less. In other words, it is a two-person game if you bet small enough. Therefore, you bet the minimum. Your probability of winning the table is .54.

If you were to lead off with a max bet, your probability of winning would be .52 if BR2 would bet the minimum. It could be even worse: If you lead off with a max bet and BR2 uses Curt's Revenge, your probability of winning drops to .40!

With these bankrolls but a different betting order, the only time you bet more than the minimum is if BR2 bets ahead of you, and bets 95 or less. In that case you should match BR2's bet.

If you bet last and both of your opponents make max bets ahead of you, make a max bet. If BR2 is not a tournament expert, your probability of winning the table is .69. If BR2 is a tournament expert who uses Curt's Revenge, your probability of winning the table is .60.

EXAMPLE 5

One Winner
Min 5
Max 500

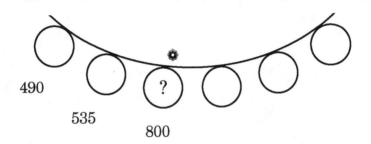

490

535

800

In this example you have a big lead over BR2. You would like to bet at least 240 to cover the situation of everybody winning, and you would like to bet no more than 260 so as to win the table if everybody loses. So if you bet first, make a bet in that range. Do not double down unless you need the extra win to beat a big-bet natural by BR2 or BR3. If BR2 is not a tournament expert, your probability of winning the table is at least .74. If BR2 is a tournament expert who uses Curt's Revenge, your probability of winning is .61.

If you bet 275 to 305, your probability of winning is .70 — if BR2 bets big. If you bet 275 and BR2 follows with a bet of 5 (which will happen if BR2 is a tournament expert), your probability of winning is only .47.

If all players bet the max, your probability of winning the table is .70.

In summary, if you bet first, bet 240 to 260. If you bet second after BR3, bet 240 to 260. If you bet second after BR2 and BR2 has bet big, bet 275 to 305. If you bet last and both BR2 and BR3 have bet big, bet from 275 to the max. If you have to make a decision in a hurry, bet the max.

EXAMPLE 6

One Winner
Min 5
Max 500

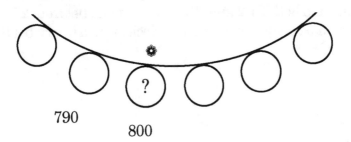

790

800

You are BR1, BR2 is close behind, and BR3 is out of it. If you bet first, bet 5 for probability of winning of .56. If you bet big, BR2 can bet small to chop your probability of winning to .49.

If you bet second, you should approximately match BR2's bet for a probability of winning of .81 if BR2 does not use Curt's Revenge, or .65 if s/he does.

EXAMPLE 7

One Winner
Min 5
Max 500

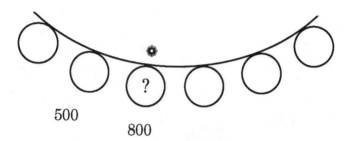

500

800

You are BR1 with a big lead over BR2, and BR3 is out of it. You can bet up to 295 without worrying that BR2 might beat you if you both lose. You would like to bet at least 205 to be able to win even if BR2 doubles the bankroll. So bet something between 205 and 295 for probability of winning of .81.

EXAMPLE 8

One Winner
Min 5
Max 500

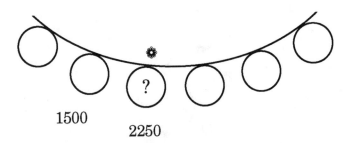

1500

2250

In this example the maximum bet is 500, and you have a lead of more than that. You can bet the minimum, in which case BR2 can beat you only by betting big, doubling the bet, and winning it. Or you can bet something over 250 so that if you win, BR2 could not beat you by doubling down, but could beat you by betting big and winning while you lose.

Bet big enough to cover a double down by BR2. If you bet something over 250, you are an 88% favorite. If you bet 5, you are a 91% favorite over a basic strategy player but only a 67% favorite over a player who doubles everything. While many of your opponents will not think of doubling everything, they probably will think of doubling enough extra times to make 255 look like a better bet than 5.

EXAMPLE 9

One Winner
Min 5
Max 500

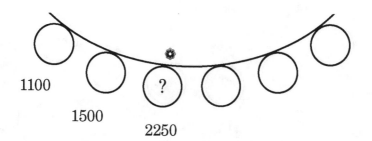

1100

1500

2250

This example differs from the preceding in that now if you bet big you give BR3 a chance to win. With a 500 max bet, the only way BR3 can beat you is to win a doubled bet while you lose a bet of over 150. Yet if you bet under 250, you give BR2 a chance to beat you by doubling down.

Your best bet is to bet big. If you bet more than 250, your probability of winning the table is .83. If you bet 5 to 145, your probability of winning the table is only .71.

EXAMPLE 10

One Winner
Min 5
Max 500

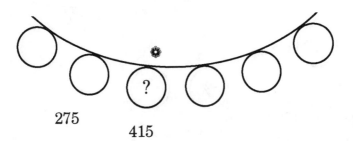

275

415

You are more than 50% ahead of BR2. (BR2's bankroll is less than 2/3 of yours.) You have the opportunity to beat BR2 both ways no matter what s/he bets. Your best bet is a third of your bankroll rounded up, or 140 in this example. If you and BR2 both win, you win the match no matter what BR2 bets. If both hands lose, you win the match no matter what BR2 bets.

EXAMPLE 11

One Winner
Min 5
Max 500

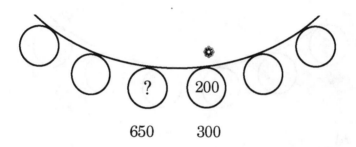

You are BR1 in a two-person game, and you bet after BR2. This is a great position to be in because you can make a bet that will give you the win if both hands win and also if both hands lose.

You should prefer to bet an amount such that after you make your bet you have a chip more than BR2 has in unbet chips. BR2 has 300 unbet, so keep 305 and bet the balance of your bankroll. Your bet turns out to be 345.

Keeping the bigger pile of unbet chips automatically gives you your best chance of beating a natural or double down by BR2. You could achieve the same result with a lot more work, but more work will not give you a better answer.

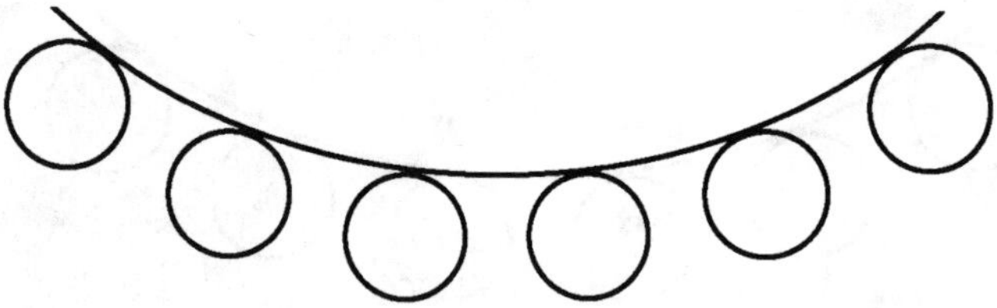

BR2 on the Final Hand

You are trying to be BR1 on the final hand, but sometimes you find yourself as BR2. As BR2, you generally bet big. You should consider betting the max, and you might also consider betting half of your bankroll and keeping the other half to double or split.

BR1 Bets Ahead of You

If BR1 makes such a large bet that you will lose if you bet the max and both hands win, but you have a chance to win by betting small, then keep one chip more than BR1 kept and bet the rest of your bankroll.

If BR1 bets more than the lead over you but not so much as to beat you if you bet the max and both hands win, then whether you bet big or small depends on BR3. If BR3 is within range of you, bet big. If BR3 is out of it, keep a chip more than BR1 has kept, and bet the rest of your bankroll.

You Bet Ahead of BR1

Your best bet is half your bankroll. (Actually, you need bet only double the amount you are behind BR1 plus a chip.)

A BR1 who is not a tournament expert most likely will follow with a small bet. If BR1 does bet small, you have a .44 probability of winning the table.

If BR1 matches your bet, use Curt's Revenge. This means if doubling your bet is your best hope to win the match, then you double down. A precise playing strategy for Curt's Revenge is explained in chapter 8. Your probability of winning the table is .38. Without Curt's Revenge, your probability of winning the table is .12 to .19.

EXAMPLE 12

One Winner
Min 5
Max 500

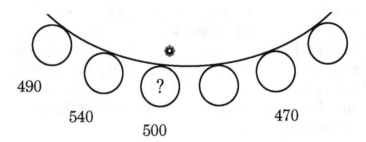

490

540

500

470

For this example, your best bet depends on whether BR1 is an experienced tournament player. If BR1 has played in a few tournaments, s/he knows to bet big because BR3 also is close enough to win. Therefore, BR1 will bet big no matter what you bet, and your best bet as BR2 is the minimum.

If BR1 is a tournament novice, s/he is likely to bet small. If BR1 does bet small, you are better off betting the max. If you bet the minimum and BR1 follows you with a minimum bet, BR1 locks you out completely. Therefore, as BR2 with a crowd in contention, if you think that BR1 might bet small, bet the max.

Betting first as BR2 is a bad position to be in. Your probability of winning the table is .18 if you bet the max and BR1 also bets the max, which is why you would rather bet more aggressively earlier and be BR1 or bust.

EXAMPLE 13

One Winner
Min 5
Max 500

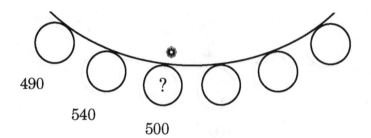

490

540

500

Three may be a crowd in a social situation; but going into the final bet of a blackjack tournament, being second out of three is much better than being second out of four. In this situation you should bet half of your bankroll. What you do for playing strategy depends on what your opponents bet. Your probability of winning the table is .28 to .32.

If you bet the max instead, your probability of winning the table is .20 if BR1 bets big and BR3 bets small.

EXAMPLE 14

One Winner
Min 5
Max 500

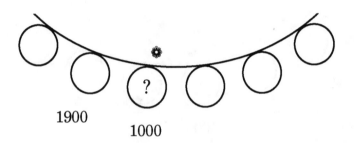

1900

1000

With a 500 maximum, this position is bleak; but it is not hopeless. Bet 500 and double your bet no matter what you get. (That means either double down or split.) Your probability of winning the table is .10 if BR1 bets more than 100, and .33 if BR1 bets less than 100.

EXAMPLE 15

One Winner
Min 5
Max 500

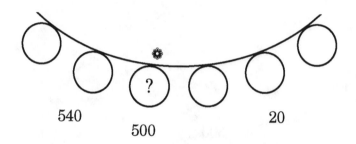

540   20

500

It is down to BR1 and yourself; BR3 is out of it. You should bet at least double the amount you are behind plus a chip, and no more than half your bankroll. That means you should bet 85 to 250.

Suppose you bet 100, just to pick a nice round number. If BR1 approximately matches your bet with a bet of 65 to 155, use Curt's Revenge and your probability of winning the table is .35. (Without Curt's Revenge, your probability of winning the table is only .19.) If BR1 bets less than 60, you win the table if you win your bet so you should play straight blackjack except you should not double down; your probability of winning is .44. If BR1 bets more than 160, you win the table if BR1 loses that bet, so you should play straight blackjack except do not double down or split; your probability of winning the table is .48.

EXAMPLE 16

One Winner
Min 5
Max 500

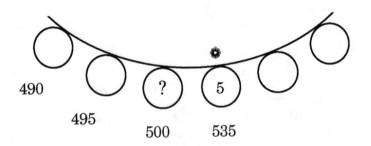

In a crowd like this, your best hope is to bet the max. If neither BR3 nor BR4 gets a natural and you win your bet, you win the table.

EXAMPLE 17

One Winner
Min 5
Max 500

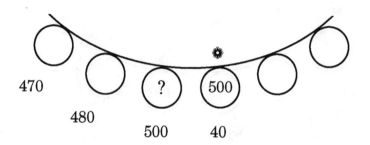

470
480
500   40
?   500

BR1 has bet so large that you cannot win if BR1's hand wins, but you can keep the most unbet chips on the table. So keep back 485, bet your other 15, and hope the dealer gets a natural.

EXAMPLE 18

One Winner
Min 5
Max 500

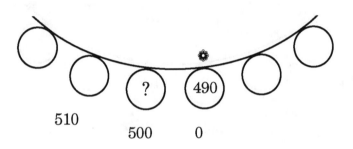

510

500   0

Your best bet here depends on whether BR1 is a tournament veteran. A BR1 who is a tournament veteran most likely will bet big to cover BR3's bet, and your best chance of winning the table is to bet small, meaning 5 to 250. (BR1's best bet is 475 or more no matter what you bet.)

If you think BR1 will bet small, as might happen if BR1 has never before played a tournament, then your best bet is 485. What makes 485 a better bet than 500 is it gives BR1 a chance to make a mistake. If BR1 tries to be smart and follow your 485 with a bet of 480 thinking to beat you by 5 if both hands win, then you can double down for less and win the table.

EXAMPLE 19

One Winner
Min 5
Max 500

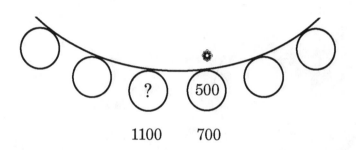

1100   700

This is a great opportunity for you. Hold back 705 or slightly more, and bet at most 395. Make a bet that allows you to win the table if both bets lose, or double down to beat a single-bet win by BR1. This is the strong variation of Curt's Revenge; it is explained more fully in chapter 8. You are the favorite though your opponent has more chips. Your probability of winning the table is .55.

EXAMPLE 20

One Winner
Min 5
Max 500

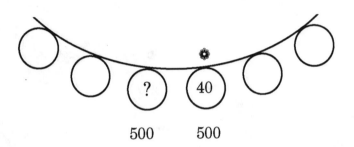

500   500

    BR1 is taking the low end; if both hands lose, BR1 wins the table. So you have no choice but to take the high end. If BR3 is within a bet of you, bet the max. Otherwise, bet at least enough to cover a double-down win by BR1, which in this example means 125 or more. Your probability of winning the table is .44.

EXAMPLE 21

One Winner
Min 5
Max 500

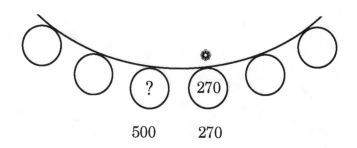

500   270

BR1 is giving you a choice of high or low. If BR3 is within reach of you, take the high end — bet the max.

If BR3 is out of it, take the low end. BR1 has bet 270, and has kept 270 unbet. So keep 275 back, and bet your remaining 225. You are the favorite in this situation. If you play straight blackjack, your probability of winning the table is .53. If you use the strong variation of Curt's Revenge, which essentially means doubling your bet in those situations where BR1 is unlikely to lose (doubling for less is fine — another 90 will do it), your probability of winning the table is .55.

EXAMPLE 22

One Winner
Min 5
Max 500

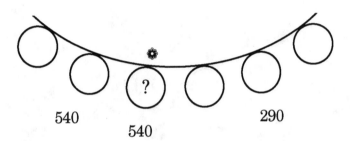

540   290

540

You are tied for the lead, and BR3 has a chance. Bet the max.

EXAMPLE 23

One Winner
Min 5
Max 500

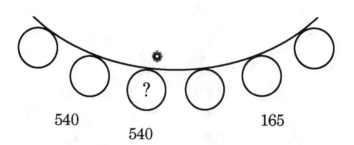

540

540

165

You are tied for the lead, and BR3 is hopelessly behind. Bet the minimum.

EXAMPLE 24

One Winner
Min 5
Max 500

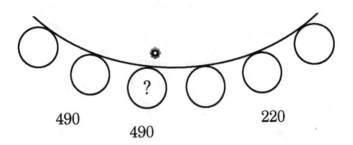

490   220

490

This example differs from the previous two in that BR3 could catch you by catching a max-bet natural. Your best bet is the same as when BR3 is hopelessly behind. With a bet of 5, you have a 49% chance of winning the table no matter what the other BR1 bets.

If you bet 490, you have a 49% chance of winning the table if the other BR1 bets small, but if that person also bets big then you have only a 34% chance because BR3 can keep the most unbet chips.

If you bet 65 to cover a natural by BR3, your probability of winning the table is .49 if the other BR1 bets 5, but only .45 if the other BR1 bets 490.

If the other BR1 bets 5 ahead of you, you are slightly better off betting from 65 to the max instead of matching the 5; each way your probability of winning the table is .49.

If the other BR1 bets anything more than 5 ahead of you, your best bet is 5.

Secret Bet

If you get to make a secret bet, save it for the last hand. Even if you bet last on the last hand and thus first on the hand before it, still keep your secret bet for the last hand. The reason is Curt's Revenge. If you bet last your opponents cannot use your bet size to determine how much to bet, but they might be able to use your bet size to decide how to play their hands.

In theory, you should be worse off when your opponents make secret bets because you have less information to use. However, that is the case only if your opponents play their secret bets perfectly. The truth is you probably are better off with secret bets than without them. One reason is you know more about what your opponents have written down for their secret bets than what they know about your secret bet. Another reason is many of your opponents do not use their secret bets at all, or use them earlier than the last hand. Some people use their secret bets on the very first hand!

When there is one winner per table, everyone who makes a secret bet tends to make a big bet. They may not bet the max, but they make bets they think of as being big. Therefore, when your opponents make secret bets, act as if you are betting after them and you know what their bets are. Occasionally you are wrong about the size of a person's secret bet, but you are right so frequently that your gains when you are right vastly outweigh your losses from being wrong.

You should do several things differently when you can make a secret bet on your last hand. You should still try to be BR1, except that you should be willing to be BR2 in a two-person game.

Secret Last Bet If You Are BR1

If it is a two-person game, bet the max minus half your lead plus a chip. If more than two people are in the fight for the top spot, either bet max minus half your lead over BR2 plus a chip, or bet the max.

The reason for making a big bet is BR2 probably will make a big bet, and you are approximately matching the bet you expect BR2 to make. You cover BR2 if s/he bets the max, and you cover BR2 if s/he bets slightly less than the max.

If BR2 doubles down or splits without busting, or if you think BR2 will double the bet (except if you think BR2 will split 10-10 against the dealer's 7 through 10 or ace), then if you can double your bet without busting you should do it. For example if you have 10-10, and BR2 has eleven and plays after you, split and do not bust. If you have 3-2 and BR2 has eleven, double down. You are not trying to beat the dealer; you are trying to beat BR2. Your initial bet puts you in the situation where you win the table if both hands win, and you win the table if both hands lose. If BR2 doubles down and you do not double your bet, then if both hands win BR2 wins the table. By doubling your own bet you preserve your win-if-both-lose, win-if-both-win position.

Here is an alternative play for a two-person game: Bet small and bluff. For example, with a lead of $800 to $700 and betting limits of $10 to $300, generally you should make a secret bet of $255. But if you think there is at least one chance in three that BR2 has made a secret bet of $10, then make a secret bet of $10. Then if you get a good hand, act happy. If BR2 has bet the minimum, you win the table regardless of the outcomes of the hands. But if BR2 in fact has bet big, then maybe s/he will reduce the chance of beating you by making a foolish double down or foolish pair split.

Secret Last Bet If You Are BR2

You should expect BR1 to bet big, and you hope to get the edge by using a modification of Curt's Revenge. So make a bet that allows you to win the table if both bets lose, and win the table if you win a doubled bet. Bet half of the max plus half of BR1's lead plus a chip. For example, with 1100 to 1150 and a 500 max, bet 280.

If BR1 does not bust, or if BR1 plays after you, double your bet if you can do so without busting. You should even split 10-10. Also double down on hard twelve and hard thirteen.

Final Comment

If you are pressed for time or bothered by the pressure or simply cannot remember the correct play, bet big. On the final hand, betting big is more likely to be correct than betting small.

CHAPTER 6
BLACKJACK:
FINAL HAND, TWO
WINNERS PER TABLE

This chapter addresses the final hand of blackjack tournaments in which there are two winners per table.

On deciding what to bet, there are only three spots worth putting yourself into:

1. High if everybody wins one bet.
2. Second high if everybody wins one bet.
3. High if everybody loses one bet.

The best way to bet the last hand depends on how many players are still in contention. Table 3 contains the rank order of preferred bets. Middle means second high if all player hands win and second high if all player hands lose.

Table 3
Desirable Spots if Two Advance

Number of Players in Contention

Bets	3	4	5 or more
best:	middle	high if all win	high if all win
2nd:	high if all lose	high if all lose	2nd high if all win
3rd:	high if all win	2nd high all win	high if all lose

Note that the only time it is advisable to try for second high if all player bets lose is if there are precisely three people in contention for the two spots. If there are more than three people in contention, do not try for second high if all player bets lose. This point is worth special mention because keeping the second-largest pile of unbet chips, which means finishing second if the dealer wipes out all player bets, seems like a reasonable thing to do. This appearance is deceiving; it may be a reasonable thing to do, but it is not the best thing to do. The problem with it is that often the dealer wipes out all bets except one, and second high drops to third high.

Last Hand, Two Players in Contention

Obviously, if you can bet the minimum and lock up one of the top two spots, then bet the minimum. Also bet the minimum if the only way you can be beaten is by BR3 getting a natural; in that case you do not have a lock, but you are at least a 96% favorite.

EXAMPLE 25

Two Winners
Min 5
Max 500

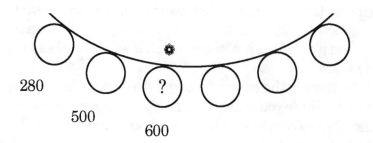

280

500

600

From your viewpoint as BR1, this is a two-person game. Bet the minimum to virtually lock out BR3. You have a 98% chance of being one of the top two.

Last Hand, Three Players in Contention

This strategy is both surprising and powerful: Go for the middle. That is, try to finish second high. Look for the opportunity to make a bet such that if all hands win you finish second high, and if all hands lose you finish second high.

Sometimes you can do better than merely getting second both ways. Sometimes you can be second high if all hands win and high if all hands lose, or vice versa. If you have a choice between those two, high if all lose and second if all win is better than high if all win and second if all lose.

Here is the easy way to get the proper bet size to control where you finish if all hands lose. Simply focus on the amount of chips not bet, and make sure you keep the second-biggest stack.

If You Are BR1

If you have a lock, bet the minimum. If you do not have a lock, keep what BR3 keeps plus at least a chip. Then if the dealer makes a hand to wipe out all bets, you finish second. If you bet first you do not know what BR2 and BR3 are going to bet, but you know they must bet something. If you keep an amount equal to BR3's bankroll, after BR3 bets you will have more chips left. If you keep one chip more, you can lose your bet and still beat a push by BR3.

If BR2 and BR3 are about equal, keep a few extra chips more so as to be keeping what BR2 keeps plus a chip.

If BR3 is way behind, keep what BR2 keeps plus a chip. (How far behind does BR3 have to be? If you keep what BR2 keeps plus a chip, all hands win, and you still finish ahead of BR3, then you have made the proper bet.)

EXAMPLE 26

Two Winners
Min 5
Max 500

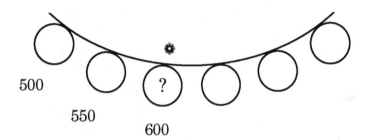

500

550

600

Keep back 505 to beat a push by BR3, and bet 95. Your probability of advancing is .71 if both of your opponents bet big, as you expect them to, or .88 if BR2 bets small.

If you were to bet 100, your probability of advancing would be .70 if both of your opponents bet big, or .85 if BR2 bets small.

If you were to bet 50, your probability of advancing would be .70 if both of your opponents bet big, or .94 if BR2 bets small.

EXAMPLE 27

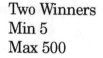

Two Winners
Min 5
Max 500

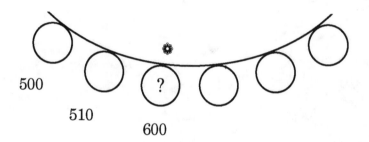

500

510

600

Your lead over BR2 is almost as large as your lead over BR3. In this case you are slightly better off keeping 515 and betting 85 for a probability of advancing of .71 (assuming both BR2 and BR3 bet big, which you expect them to do). If you bet 90 or 95, your probability of advancing is .70. If you bet 100, your probability of advancing is .69.

EXAMPLE 28

Two Winners
Min 5
Max 500

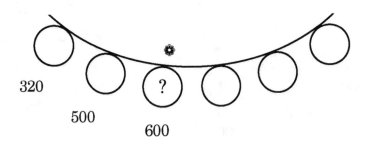

BR3 is almost out of it, but not quite. If you keep 505 and bet 95, your probability of advancing is .93. Betting 45 has the same .93 probability of advancing. If you keep 500 and bet 100, your probability of advancing is .92. If you keep 320 and bet 280, your probability of advancing is .91. If you bet 10, your probability of advancing is only .71. These numbers assume your opponents bet big.

If you bet 275 your probability of advancing is .92 if your opponents bet big, but only .87 if BR2 holds back a chip more than you.

EXAMPLE 29

Two Winners
Min 5
Max 500

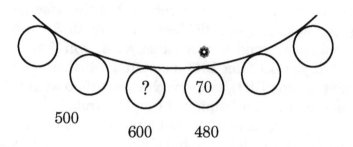

Hold back either 485 to beat what BR2 has unbet or 505 to beat what BR3 has. If you bet 95, your probability of advancing is .93. If you bet 115, your probability of advancing is .91.

If You Are BR2

If BR1 has first place locked up, then it is you against BR3 for second place. This reduces to a two-person game with one winner, so the strategy of the previous chapter applies.

If you are in a three-person game and BR1 does not have first place locked up, try for the middle. (Again the qualifier: This is a three-person game. Second high if all hands lose is not a good target if there are more than three players with a chance to advance.) If you have to bet first, bet the amount you are behind BR1 plus a few more chips; you are hoping BR1 bets small and BR3 bets big, so you have second place whether you all win or all lose.

If you bet after BR3 (no matter whether you bet before or after BR1), keep one chip more than what BR3 keeps, and bet the balance of your bankroll.

If you bet before BR3 but after BR1, try to bet just enough to beat BR1 by a chip if you both win your bets. If you do not have enough chips to make that bet, do the following two calculations and keep whichever is smaller: Consider keeping what BR3 has for a bankroll plus a chip, and consider keeping what BR1 keeps plus a chip; keeping the smaller amount means making the larger bet.

EXAMPLE 30

Two Winners
Min 5
Max 500

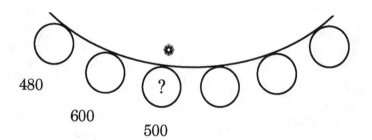

480

600

500

Bet at least 150, and maybe 200 or 250. You are hoping BR1 bets small after you.

EXAMPLE 31

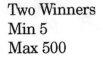

Two Winners
Min 5
Max 500

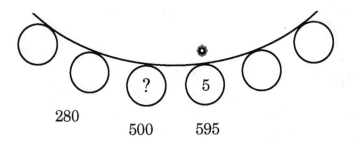

280

500   595

If you bet slightly more than 110, you are high if all hands win and second if all hands lose; your probability of advancing is .86.

EXAMPLE 32

Two Winners
Min 5
Max 500

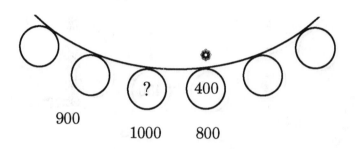

BR1 has made a huge bet, and the amount of chips s/he has left is less than BR3's bankroll. With a 500 max, you cannot bet enough to beat BR1 if you both win your bets. Therefore, keep what BR1 keeps plus a chip. Hold back 805 and bet 195 for a probability of advancing of .83 if BR3 bets big, and .67 if s/he bets small.

A bet of 95 would give you a probability of advancing of .68 if BR3 bets big, as s/he should and probably would.

EXAMPLE 33

Two Winners
Min 5
Max 500

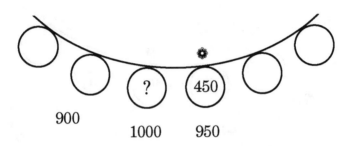

This example differs from the previous one in that now BR1 has unbet chips greater than BR3's bankroll. In this case it does not matter whether you focus on BR1 or BR3. With a bet of either 45 or 95, your probability of advancing is .63.

If you bet 500, your probability of advancing is .75 if BR3 bets big, but only .54 if BR3 bets small. So if you know BR3 is going to bet big, bet 500 and take the middle.

EXAMPLE 34

Two Winners
Min 5
Max 500

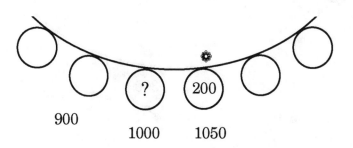

In this example you can make a bet big enough to beat BR1 if you both win. That is your best bet. Most likely BR3 will bet 450 after you. If you bet 455 or more, your probability of advancing is .79.

If you bet 45, your probability of advancing is .68.

If you bet 95, your probability of advancing is .64.

EXAMPLE 35

Two Winners
Min 5
Max 500

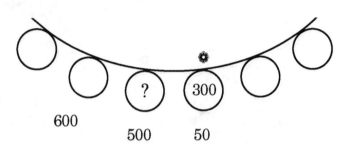

BR3 has 50 unbet, so keep 55 unbet; that means you bet 445. Your probability of advancing is .80.

If you were to bet half of your bankroll, your probability of advancing would be only .70.

If You Are BR3

If you bet first, definitely bet more than the amount you are behind BR2, and if possible bet more than the amount you are behind BR1. Consider betting the max.

If you bet after one of the leaders, try to make a bet that gives you second high if all bets lose; whatever that person keeps, you keep plus one chip. (Again the word of caution: This strategy is for three-person games only.) If the person betting ahead of you has bet too small for you to do that, bet enough to beat that person if you both win.

If you bet last in a three-person game, look for the opportunity to get the middle. You can actually be the favorite to advance if you can make a bet that will make you second high if all hands win and second high if all hands lose. The way to do it is keep the second-most unbet chips on the table.

EXAMPLE 36

Two Winners
Min 5
Max 500

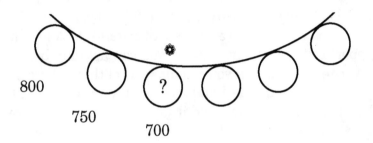

800

750

700

The important thing here is to bet more than 100. A bet of no more than 350 will keep the option of splitting.

EXAMPLE 37

Two Winners
Min 5
Max 500

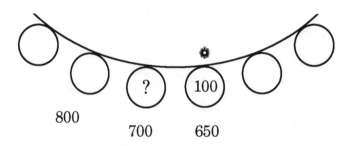

If you bet less than 50, BR1 will be able to lock up
a spot by betting the minimum, and you will have second
if all bets lose and third if all bets win. Over 50 but less
than 150 is worse—you will have third if all bets win and
third if all bets lose. If you bet over 150 you will have first
or second if all bets win, and probably third if all bets lose.

It turns out that your probability of advancing is .48
with a bet of 5 and .50 with a bet of 350. So you are slightly
better off with 350. Note that you should bet 350 and not
155 in order to cover a natural by BR2.

EXAMPLE 38

Two Winners
Min 5
Max 500

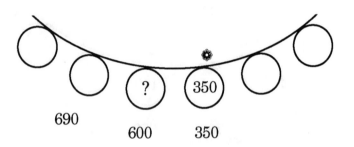

BR1 has kept 350 back. Keep 355 back, betting 245 and beating BR1 if you both lose. Your probability of advancing is .59.

If you were to bet 455, your probability of advancing would be .48.

EXAMPLE 39

Two Winners
Min 5
Max 500

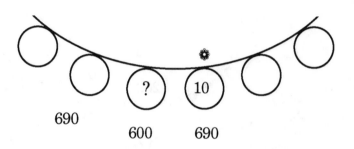

BR1 has kept 690 unbet, and you do not have that many chips. So bet more than 120 to beat BR1 if you both win. Your probability of advancing is only .48, but that is the best you can do.

EXAMPLE 40

Two Winners
Min 5
Max 500

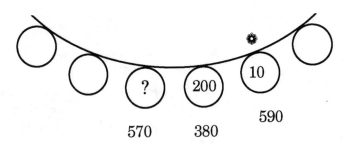

570   380

You may be BR3, but you have got the upper hand due to betting last. Any bet between 55 and 185 will give you second if all hands win and second if all hands lose. Your probability of advancing is .80.

Your bet size is easy to figure. The chips left in front of your opponents total 590 and 380; this is what they will end up with if all hands lose. You want to keep more than 380 in front of you, which means betting as much as 185. No more thinking is needed — just shove out the 185.

Betting 55 gives no higher probability of advancing than betting 185 so you do not need the 55 number to make a decision on how much to bet. But here is how you get it anyhow. If all hands win, your opponents will have 610 and 780. You need to bet only 45 to be second in that event. But you can bet more than 45 with no problem, so you might as well cover a double down by BR1. If BR1 wins a doubled bet, s/he would end up with 620. You would need to win 55 to get ahead of BR1. That is how you get the 55.

Last Hand, Four or More Players in Contention

This section assumes that BR4 still has a shot at advancing to the next round. If you are BR1 you have got a good chance to advance. If you are not BR1, about the only thing you can do is bet the max; if you win the hand you may advance, and if you lose the hand you probably will not advance.

You Are BR1 And You Bet First

There are two possibilities for how much to bet. Calculate both and use the larger. One possibility is to keep back an amount of chips equal to one more than what BR3 has for a bankroll, and bet the balance of your bankroll. The other possibility is to calculate what BR4 would have with a max-bet win, and bet enough to beat that.

EXAMPLE 41

Two Winners
Min 5
Max 500

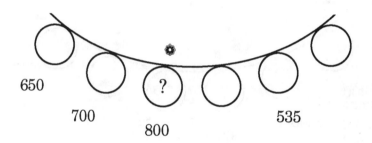

650

700

800

?

535

The two bets to consider are 145 to hold back a chip more than what BR3 has, and 240 to beat what BR4 would have with a max-bet win. 240 is larger than 145, so bet 240. Your probability of advancing is .61. Had you bet 145, your probability of advancing would have been .57. These numbers assume your opponents bet big; if one or more of them bets small, your probability of advancing is greater and 240 is still your best bet.

355, to cover a max-bet win by BR3, is inferior to 240 no matter what your opponents bet.

EXAMPLE 42

Two Winners
Min 5
Max 500

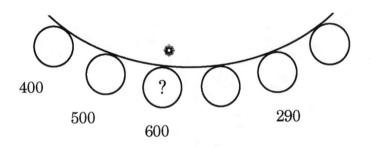

400

500

600

?

290

BR4 exists, but the best s/he can do with a max-bet win is get up to 580; you have got that covered no matter what you bet. So bet 195, keeping back a chip more than BR3's bankroll. Your probability of advancing is .75 if your opponents all bet big as you expect them to, and .80 if BR2 bets small.

If you bet 200 instead of 195, you are 1% worse off.

If you bet less than 20, you can lock out BR4 and make it a three-person game; but your probability of advancing is .69 if your opponents all bet big as you expect them to, and .98 if BR2 bets small.

If you bet 100 and keep back 500 to match BR2, your probability of advancing is .66 if your opponents all bet big, and .88 if BR2 bets small.

EXAMPLE 43

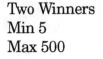

Two Winners
Min 5
Max 500

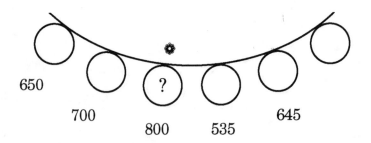

650

700

800   535

645

The bets the general rule says to consider are 145 to keep a chip more than BR3's bankroll, and 350 to beat a max-bet win by BR4. 350 is larger, so the better bet is 350. Your probability of advancing is .62 if all of your opponents bet big, or .65 if BR2 bets small as you expect to happen.

This is an example of a situation in which you might notice that you have a better bet than what the general rule recommends. You can cover a max-bet win by BR3 by betting only slightly larger than 350. Losing 355 is the same to you as losing 350, but winning 355 instead of 350 turns a possible push into a possible win. If you bet 355 your probability of advancing is .70 if all of your opponents bet big, and .66 if BR2 bets small as you expect to happen.

If you bet 145 your probability of advancing is .49 if all of your opponents bet big, and .45 if BR2 bets small.

If you bet 95 your probability of advancing is .50 if all of your opponents bet big, and .55 if BR2 bets small.

You Are BR1 And You Do Not Bet First

This section assumes four or more people are still in contention on the last hand. Finding your optimal bet is complicated and time-consuming. You do not have much time for deciding how much to bet, and you are under too much pressure to do any complicated arithmetic. So here is a rule of thumb that you can use quickly and accurately. It yields one of your best bets, though possibly not your very best bet.

The rule of thumb is to keep the second-largest pile of unbet chips and bet the balance of your bankroll. Thus if the dealer gets a natural and wipes out all hands, you finish second; and if the dealer does not wipe out all hands, you have got a large enough bet going to have a good chance to be one of the top two if you win your hand.

EXAMPLE 44

Two Winners
Min 5
Max 500

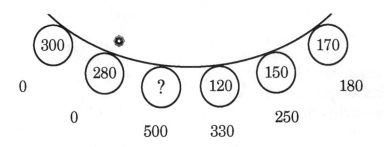

0

0   500   330   250   180

Keeping the second-most unbet chips means making a bet of 245 and having a probability of advancing of .63. Here is an instance where you might notice an opportunity to make a better bet. If all of your opponents win single bets, the most any of them will end up with is 600. So you do not really need to bet as high as 245; a bet of 105 will win the table if you all win your bets. If you bet 105, your probability of advancing is .72.

EXAMPLE 45

Two Winners
Min 5
Max 500

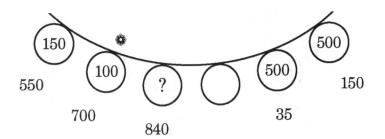

Your best bet is 285. You get this number by noting that BR2 has 700 unbet, BR3 has 550 unbet, and all other opponents have less than 550 unbet. So keep 555 unbet, and bet the balance of your bankroll, which just happens to be 285. This bet gives you a .67 chance of advancing to the next round.

Keeping the most unbet chips and betting the balance of 135 would give you a probability of .60 of advancing to the next round.

If you bet 315, your best bet-first bet, your probability of advancing to the next round would be .49.

You Are Not BR1

This section assumes four or more people in contention. Here too there is a rule of thumb that is not perfect, but is quick and yields excellent decisions. Keep the largest pile of unbet chips if you can. If you do not have that many chips, bet the max.

EXAMPLE 46

Two Winners
Min 5
Max 500

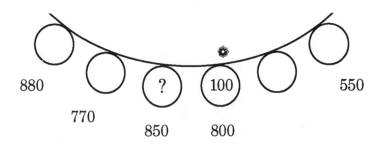

880

770

850

?

100

800

550

Look around the table to see what is the most unbet chips anyone has. You see BR1 with 800 left, but BR2 has yet to bet from a bankroll of 880. You have less than 880, so bet the max. Do not keep the second most unbet chips because you are not BR1 and this is not a three-person game.

Secret Bet

If you get to make a secret bet, save it for the last hand. When there are two winners per table, if BR1 makes a secret bet it tends to be a small bet. Everyone else who makes a secret bet tends to make a big bet. They may not bet the max, but they make bets they think of as being big. Therefore, when your opponents make secret bets, act as if you are betting after them and you know what their bets are.

EXAMPLE 47

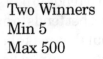

Two Winners
Min 5
Max 500

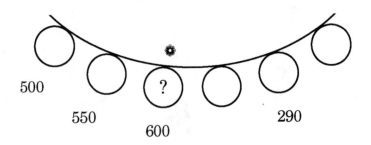

500

550

600

290

If you had to make a bet your opponents could see, you should bet 95. But suppose you can make a secret bet. Your opponents most likely will make bets they consider large, which in this case probably means 200 to 250 or so. So bet 200 yourself. If these predictions of their bet sizes are correct, then you are high if all hands win and high if all hands lose; and your probability of advancing to the next round is .82.

CHAPTER 7

BLACKJACK: FINAL HAND, THREE WINNERS PER TABLE

This chapter addresses blackjack tournaments in which the top three money winners from the table advance to the next round.

You might think that if six players sit down at a table and three of them are going to advance to the next round, you should easily be one of the top three if you are a skillful blackjack player. Such is not the case. You have a slightly better chance than your opponents of being one of the top three, but you may not make it.

If you have to make a catch-up bet, it is best to try to get ahead of BR2. Going into the final hand, being BR2 is better than being BR3 on the basis of probability of winning compared to bankroll. That is, being BR1 or BR2 is more efficient than being BR3.

On the last hand, try to keep the third-highest amount of unbet chips, and bet the balance of your bankroll. That should put you in the position where if all players win their bets you finish in the top three, and if all lose you finish in the top three.

EXAMPLE 48

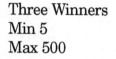

Three Winners
Min 5
Max 500

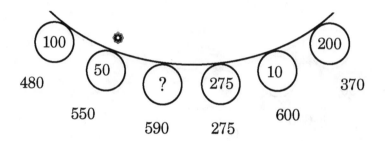

Bet 105 because the 485 you have unbet gives you the third-largest amount of unbet chips. If all players win their bets, you will finish third high. If all player bets lose, you will finish third high. Your probability of advancing to the next round is .59.

EXAMPLE 49

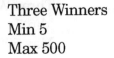

Three Winners
Min 5
Max 500

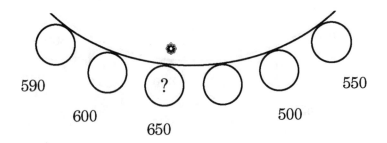

590   550
600   500
650

You would like to make a bet such that you are in the top three if all bets win and in the top three if all bets lose. That is difficult to do when you bet first. Your best bet is the middle of what you think your opponents are likely to bet. In this case a good bet would be 100 to 150.

If you bet too large, your opponents will make bets such that you will finish first if all bets win, but fourth or worse if all bets lose. You want to be third or better if all bets lose.

If you bet too small, your opponents will make bets such that you will finish first if all bets lose, but fourth or worse if all bets win. You want to be third or better if all bets win.

EXAMPLE 50

Three Winners
Min 5
Max 500

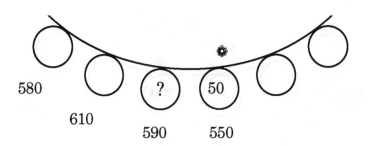

Here again you want to be in the top three if all bets win and also if all bets lose. BR2 led off with a bet that was too small, so you should bet enough to beat BR2 if you both win. The number 65 comes to mind. Most likely BR4 will come up with a big bet to give you the middle position you want.

EXAMPLE 51

Three Winners
Min 5
Max 500

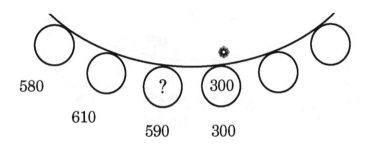

In this example, BR2 has led off with too large a bet. Your best chance of finishing in the top three both ways is to hold back more than BR2 has held back. BR2 has 300 unbet, so you should hold back 305, betting 285. You expect either or both of the players betting after you to bet small, giving you the middle.

Of course if you think that both players betting after you will bet large, then bet 315 instead of 285. However, experience shows that players bet much more conservatively when three people advance than when only one or two advance.

CHAPTER 8 BLACKJACK PLAYING STRATEGIES

Of course you should not double down if you can afford to lose a single bet but not a doubled bet. And you should not double down if you do not need to win that much money to win the table and you might want to take a fourth card. There are other instances when you should deviate from normal (non-tournament) play.

Push Is as Bad as Loss

If a push is as bad as a loss, you should deviate from basic strategy in the following ways: Stand on twelve against 2 or 3, stand on sixteen against 8 or 9, stand on fifteen or more against 10, and hit soft eighteen against 8 and against ace.

No Doubling or Splitting

If you do not double or split, because you have bet all the rest of your bankroll or do not want to risk the extra money, then you are worse off compared to using basic strategy. Refusing to double or split costs you about 2% in a one-deck game, and about 1.8% in a six-deck game.

Probabilities For One Hand of Blackjack

With no doubling or splitting, the probabilities for one hand of basic strategy are as shown in table 4.

Table 4
Probability of Win, Push, Lose

One Player:

win	.44
push	.08
lose	.48

Two Players:

both win	.30
either or both win	.58
A wins and B pushes	.02
A wins and B loses	.12
both push	.01
A pushes and B loses	.05
both lose	.31

Win Both Ways

If it is the last hand, you are BR1, and you win the table if BR2 and you have the same outcome, then you should deviate from normal hit/stand strategy in certain situations. If you do not know what BR2 has for cards: You should stand on sixteen against 9, and you stand on fifteen or sixteen against 10. If you know what BR2 has, you should play according to table 5. The rows for 16 and under are for use only when BR2 has yet to play the hand. If BR2 has played the hand already and has stood on a hand of less than seventeen, then use the "stood stiff" row.

Table 5
BR1 Stands On These Totals If
Win Both Ways

BR2 has	*Dealer's Upcard*									
	2	3	4	5	6	7	8	9	10	Ace
21	14	14	13	13	13	17	17	17	17	17
20	14	13	13	12	13	17	17	17	17	17
19	13	13	12	12	12	17	17	17	15	17
18	12	12	12	12	12	17	17	13	13	17
17	12	12	12	12	12	16	12	12	12	14
stood stiff	12	12	12	12	12	12	12	12	12	12
16	13	12	12	12	12	17	17	16	15	17
15	13	12	12	12	12	17	17	16	15	17
14	13	12	12	12	12	17	17	16	15	17
13	13	12	12	12	12	17	17	16	15	17
12	13	12	12	12	12	17	17	16	15	17
11	13	13	12	12	12	17	17	17	16	17
10	13	13	12	12	12	17	17	17	16	17
9	13	12	12	12	12	17	17	16	14	17
8	12	12	12	12	12	17	17	14	14	17
7	12	12	12	12	12	17	15	14	13	17
6	13	12	12	12	12	17	17	16	15	17
5	13	12	12	12	12	17	17	16	15	17
4	13	12	12	12	12	17	17	16	15	17
soft 18	12	12	12	12	12	17	17	15	15	17
soft 17	12	12	12	12	12	17	16	15	14	17
soft 16	13	13	12	12	12	17	17	17	16	17
soft 15	13	13	12	12	12	17	17	17	16	17
soft 14	13	13	12	12	12	17	17	17	16	17
soft 13	13	13	12	12	12	17	17	17	16	17
unknown	13	12	12	12	12	17	17	16	15	17

Insure If Lose Both Ways

If your opponent has you in the uncomfortable position where you lose the table if you both win your bets, and you lose the table if you both lose your bets, then take a little bit of insurance if the dealer has an ace up. This gives your opponent the opportunity to make a mistake. Your opponent's correct play is to match your insurance bet, but s/he may not realize it. For example, suppose you have 600 out of which you have bet 300, and your opponent who plays after you has 650 and also bets 300. If the dealer shows an ace, you should take at least 30 of insurance. (You win 2:1 on your insurance bet if the dealer has a natural, and you are behind by 50. That means you need to insure for more than 25.)

Double Anything

Sometimes you want to double your bet no matter what you get. The pairs you should split are different from normal basic strategy because many pair splits end up with a loser and a winner for a push overall. If the reason you are doubling your bet is you need to win both bets, you do not want a push. When you do split a pair, you should stand on any stiff because your best chance of winning both bets is by the dealer busting.

Here are the pairs you should split when you need a double win and a push is not good enough. Always split ace-ace, 2-2, 3-3, 8-8, 9-9, and 10-10. Split 6-6 and 7-7 against 2-6. Split 7-7 against 10. If one deck is used, split 7-7 against 9. With any other pair, for example with 7-7 against 7, double down rather than split.

With this strategy, your probability of winning is .33, your probability of pushing is .08, and your probability of losing is .59.

Curt's Revenge

This strategy is named after Anthony Curtis because I got the idea for it while watching him play blackjack in a tournament. This was the situation. Curtis trailed by $250, and bet $500 on the last hand. BR1 matched his $500 bet. Curtis received nineteen, BR1 received seventeen, and I was hoping the dealer would end up with seventeen, eighteen, or nineteen to make Curtis the winner of the match. The dealer hit to twenty, so Curtis lost.

Then I started to think about what Curtis should have done had he gotten the seventeen and BR1 gotten the nineteen. Standing on seventeen would have meant losing the match for certain. Hitting would have done no good unless he hit to twenty and the dealer got nineteen or twenty, or he hit to twenty-one and the dealer got nineteen, twenty, or twenty-one. I realized that doubling down was better than hitting because then Curtis would win the match if he won his hand. For example, doubling down and catching an ace for eighteen would win the match for Curtis if the dealer busted or finished with seventeen or eighteen. By simply hitting seventeen and catching an ace, Curtis would still have a loser and would have to hit it again.

Thus Curt's Revenge means doubling the bet for the best chance to win the match. Use it on the last hand of play if winning a doubled bet is enough to win the match, but winning a single bet is not enough.

Use the pair splits from the doubling on anything strategy. That means splitting ace-ace, 2-2, 3-3, 8-8, 9-9, and 10-10 no matter what the dealer shows. Split 6-6 and 7-7 against 2-6. Split 7-7 against 10. And split 7-7 against 9 if one deck is being used, but double down in a multiple-deck game.

On any soft total you should double down. If you get a natural and it pays enough to win the match for you, stand on it. If the natural does not pay enough to win the match for you, double down on it.

There are two situations in which you should not double down. One is if BR1 has played ahead of you and has busted. The other is if you have a hard total of eighteen or nineteen and BR1 has less. For example, with hard seventeen you should double down unless BR1 has busted. With hard nineteen, you should double down if BR1 has nineteen, twenty, or twenty-one, but if BR1 has anything else you stand.

Your probability of winning your hand is .40 if you play after BR1, and .38 if you play ahead of BR1.

If you cannot see BR1's cards, double down on hard seventeen or less and on any soft hand for a probability of winning of .38.

Since Curt's Revenge is a losing strategy by normal blackjack standards, doubling for less makes sense.

Similar Situations

Try to be alert for similar situations. For example, here is one that happened to me. It was the last hand, two players were advancing to the next round, and I was BR2. We all made max bets. BR3 got a natural, putting him ahead of me if I won but a single bet. BR1 had fourteen. The dealer showed a 3. I had 10-10.

If I stood: I would finish as BR2 if the dealer hit to seventeen, eighteen, nineteen, or twenty; I would finish as BR3 if the dealer busted or hit to twenty-one. By standing I had about a .51 probability of finishing as BR2.

If I split my 10-10: I would finish as BR* if the dealer busted and I did not; I would also finish as BR* if the dealer made a hand and I beat it with either of my hands, or if I pushed with both of my hands.

My probability of finishing as BR* was better by splitting my 10s. The dealer had about a .38 probability of busting. The probability of the dealer making a hand and me beating it with at least one of my hands was about .34. So I had about a .72 probability of finishing as BR* by splitting my 10-10, compared with a .51 by standing pat.

Strong Variation of Curt's Revenge

Sometimes as BR2 you bet after BR1, and you can make a bet such that if both hands lose, you win the table. But if it looks as though BR1 is likely to win a bet, then you must win a doubled bet to win the table.

For example, BR1 has 400 and bets 200; you have 380 and bet 170. If you both lose, you win the table with 210 to 200. By winning the hand, BR1 ends up with 600 and you must win a doubled bet to finish ahead.

This is the strong variation of Curt's Revenge. In the strong variation, if you both lose single bets, you win the table. In the ordinary version of Curt's Revenge, if you both lose single bets you lose the table.

If BR1 busts, you should not double or split. The better hand BR1 has, the more likely you are to double down or split a pair.

Table 6 identifies the hands you should double and split as BR2 when the strong variation of Curt's Revenge is appropriate.

Table 6
Strong Form of Curt's Revenge

Dealer's Upcard

BR1's Hand	2	3	4	5	6	7	8	9	10	ace
Hard Hands To Be Doubled										
21	all	all	all	all	all	all	all	all	all	all
20	5-17	5-17	5-18	5-18	5-18	all	all	all	5-17	7-18
19	5-14	5-14	5-14	5-16	5-16	all	5-18	9-11	9-11	9-11
18	8-11	8-11	6-11	5-12	5-13	7-16	9-11	none	none	none
17	reg	reg	reg	reg	reg	reg	none	none	none	none
stiff	reg	reg	reg	reg	reg	none	none	none	none	none
Soft Hands To Be Doubled										
21	all	all	all	all	all	all	all	all	all	all
20	all	all	all	all	all	all	all	all	all	all
19	all	all	all	all	all	all	all	all	20	17-20
18	all	all	all	all	all	all	18-20	none	none	none
17	20	19-20	17-20	18-20	18-20	19-20	none	none	none	none
stiff	none	none	20	18-20	18-20	none	none	none	none	none

Table 6 Continued

Pairs To Be Split

21	all	all	all	all	all	all	all	all	all	all
20	all	all	all	all	all	all	all	all	all	all
19	all	all	all	all	all	all	1-3, 8-10	1,10	1-4, 8-10
18	reg	reg	all	all	all	all	reg	reg	reg
17	reg	reg	reg	reg	reg	reg	reg	reg	reg
stiff	reg	reg	reg	reg	reg	reg	reg	reg	reg

KEY

all: double all hands or split all pairs except double down on 4-4 and 5-5.

none: do not double down.

reg: regular; e.g. basic strategy.

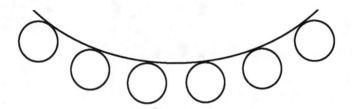

CHAPTER 9
BLACKJACK:
MATCH PLAY

This chapter applies to match-play blackjack, which is you against one other person, playing the same cards at the same table, with only one of you advancing in the tournament. The format is interesting. Each player makes a bet. One player hand is dealt, and each player plays it as s/he wishes, using buttons to indicate hit, stand, double, split, or surrender. Though each player plays the same cards, the outcomes can be different due to different bets and different actions on the cards. The players bet and play in order, with the order switching from hand to hand.

You have got a huge edge if you are BR1 going into the last hand, so part of your strategy is maneuvering to be BR1 at that time. What you do on that last hand also is critical.

Seat Selection

Playing last on the final hand is an advantage. If you can figure out which seat acts second on the final hand, and if you get to choose your seat, try to get the one that gives you the edge.

In the Early Going

Bet the minimum and play basic strategy. If you can count cards, bet in accordance with the count and use the appropriate playing strategy. Hopefully, your opponent's mistakes will give you a lead.

If your opponent is betting wildly, do not worry about falling behind. But if your opponent bets big, gets a lead, and then bets small, you have got to go after him or her.

You Are BR1 And You Bet First

If your opponent is not a skillful tournament player, you can afford to ignore him or her.

But if you recognize your opponent as being a skillful tournament player, try to keep the lead. Bet an amount less than your lead. You can bet more than the minimum if doing so will make it more difficult for your opponent to make a bet that will catch you. If your opponent is a card counter, and the count is good, and your lead is small, you might bet an amount equal to a chip greater than your lead.

You Are BR1 And You Bet Second

The important thing is to keep the lead. Approximately match your opponent's bet. Bet an amount such that if the player hand wins you keep your lead, and if the player hand loses you keep your lead.

You Are BR2 And You Bet First

Your best bet is the minimum. If you are counting cards, bet in accordance with the count.

You Are BR2 And You Bet Second

You would like to get a swing, but you do not have to get it all in one hand. If BR1 bets more than the minimum, you probably should bet the minimum. If BR1 bets the minimum and you are counting cards and the count is high enough to give you an edge, bet more than the minimum.

If you can play the hand differently than BR1 plays it without making a bad play, do it.

In the Late Going

You want to get the lead, and once you have got it you want to keep it.

If You Are Behind

Try to take the lead by getting a sufficient difference in bets. For example, if you are 20 behind and your opponent bets 50, you should bet either less than 30 or more than 70. Losing hands are more common than winning hands so it is easier to get a swing by betting less than your opponent bets, hoping that both bets lose to put you ahead in the match. But if your opponent bets small, then bet big enough so that if both bets win you are ahead in the match. Make your catch-up bet when you are betting second, and play your normal game when you are betting first.

If you need a bigger swing than what you can get with the difference in bets, be willing to play the hand differently than your opponent plays it, hoping s/he loses while you win. For example, suppose you are behind 300 to 100, your opponent bets 50, and you follow with your whole 100. If the player hand is sixteen against 8 and your opponent signals for a hit, you stand. If your opponent signals stand, you hit. If you luck out and win while your opponent loses, you are behind by only 250 to 200.

If You Are Ahead

The value of your lead increases in steps at half-max-bet intervals. Max bet means the most your opponent can bet. Your probability of winning the match is approximately the same whether you have a lead of one chip or almost half a max bet; but if your lead is more than half a max bet, then your probability of winning goes up significantly. Therefore, if you are ahead by less than half a max bet, you should be willing to jeopardize almost all of your lead in attempt to stretch your lead to half a max bet. Likewise, if you are ahead by more than half a max bet but less than a max bet, you should be willing to jeopardize part of your lead to try to get a full max bet ahead.

When you have the lead and you bet first, bet up to the amount of your lead less a chip or up to half the amount of your opponent's bankroll, whichever is less. Make a bet that gives your opponent the most difficulty in overtaking you.

Whenever you play second, make a bet such that whether it wins or loses you will still have the lead. The easiest thing is to simply match your opponent's bet.

If your opponent makes a huge bet, figure out if you can make a bet such that you will have more than twice as many chips left if the player hand loses, and still be ahead if the player hand wins. For example, if you are leading by 700 to 500 and your opponent bets 250, hold back 510 and bet 190. If both bets lose, you are ahead 510 to 250, which is a huge lead at matchplay blackjack. If both bets win, you are still ahead, but only 890 to 750.

An extreme example is if your opponent bets ahead of you, and goes all in. Keep back one chip and bet the rest of your bankroll. Then play the cards exactly the same way your opponent plays them. If the player hand loses, the match is over and you win, one chip to zero. If the player hand wins, your opponent's bankroll is doubled and yours is almost doubled; therefore, your opponent is no better off if the player hand wins, but is considerably worse off if the player hand loses.

If your opponent has made a huge bet but you cannot keep more than twice as many chips as s/he keeps and still stay ahead if the player hand wins, do the arithmetic to see if you can keep back 50% more than your opponent keeps back and still stay ahead if the player hand wins. If you cannot stay ahead with a win of that bet, or if you cannot do the arithmetic due to time constraints or pressure, then simply match your opponent's bet. For example, suppose you are leading by 600 to 500 and your opponent bets 250. Do not hold back 510 and bet 90, because if the player hand wins you are BR2. It is better to hold back 380 and bet 220; you would prefer to see the player hand lose, because then you have a lead of more than half a max bet. Alternatively, bet 250 to match your opponent's bet.

In the late going, also match your opponent's play of the cards. If your opponent misplays a hand, you misplay it the same way to maintain your lead.

Third-Last Hand

If you get only one secret bet, save it for the final hand no matter whether you play first or second. If you get two secret bets, use the first one when you have to bet first on the third-last or second-last hand. If you have the option of passing a hand (equivalent to a bet of zero), consider making a secret pass.

If you bet second, you are BR2, and BR1 makes a secret bet, bet enough to get the swing you need. Act as if BR1 has bet zero. If you bet second, you are BR2, and BR1 does not make a secret bet, of course you make a bet that will give you the swing you need.

If you bet second and you are BR1, try to match BR2's bet.

Second-Last Hand

If you have two secret bets and you bet first, use a secret bet.

If you are BR2, bet the max.

If you are BR1, try to match BR2's bet.

Last Hand

If it is allowed, make a secret bet. Your opponent probably will make a secret bet also.

Blair's Lock

Suppose you are ahead by 1070 to 500, the max bet is 500, and you must bet and play first. You have a lock if you make the correct bet and play the hand correctly. Try to solve this one yourself.

If you bet too small, your opponent could get a natural on a bet of 500 and beat you. If the player hand is not a natural, your opponent will hit if you stand or stand if you hit; thus if s/he wins a max bet and you lose too much, you lose the match.

The solution is to bet 130, and if the player hand is not a natural you surrender. Even twenty against 5 you surrender. You finish with 1005 and the most your opponent can end up with is 1000. This strategy was first devised by Blair Rodman, a tournament expert.

The break-even point for Blair's Lock is your bankroll must be more than 17/8 of BR2's bankroll. If BR2's bankroll is not exactly divisible by 8, you might have to have a chip or two more. The appropriate bet is double the amount by which your lead exceeds one max bet, less a chip.

A Variation Of Blair's Lock

You are BR1, you bet first on the final hand, and BR2 has no secret bet left. You can bet just less than twice your lead, and surrender if your opponent passes or bets the minimum. For example: If you are ahead by 1200 to 960, you can bet up to 475. If BR2 passes, simply surrender no matter what you get to lock up a victory. You must bet enough to cover a max-bet double down by BR2, which in this example means betting at least 370. The easiest bet to remember is double your lead less a chip.

You Have a Virtual Lock

Play as if you have a lock if you have more than double BR2's chips. Play as if you have a lock if you are more than two max bets ahead of BR2. Bet the minimum. (With secret bets and passes, make a secret pass.)

For example, suppose you are ahead by 850 to 400. Your best bet is pass. Your opponent wins the match with a big-bet natural, but you are a 96% favorite.

You Are Ahead By More Than a Max Bet But You Do Not Have a Lock

This section assumes that either you are betting first or your opponent has made a secret bet. Obviously if you are betting and playing second and your opponent has not made a secret bet, you have a lock if you mimic your opponent's bet and play.

Bet enough to win if your opponent doubles down. Example: With 1200 to 650, bet at least 105. With 1800 to 1200 bet at least 405. An easy rule of thumb that gets a good bet is you bet the max or half of the amount of your opponent's bankroll, whichever is less.

You Are Ahead By At Least a Half Bet

Bet a chip less than the amount of your lead. Thus if you lose and your opponent passes, you win the match.

Your opponent probably has thought of passing or betting the minimum and doubling down on a foolish total, hoping you will double down and bust. So if your opponent doubles down and you know that s/he knows it was a bad play, just hit instead of doubling. In other words, play your opponent for having bet so small that if you double down and lose you will pass him or her going backwards.

You Are Ahead By Less Than Half a Max Bet

Bet an amount large enough to beat a max-bet win by your opponent. Do that even if your opponent has been making small bets the whole way; assume your opponent is willing to make a big bet when s/he has to.

Bet an amount equal to your opponent's bankroll less 2/3 of your lead plus a chip. (This is the minimum you must bet to defeat a natural.) If that is too complicated to figure under pressure, bet an amount equal to BR2's bankroll less your lead plus a chip (though this will not beat a natural by your opponent). Follow your opponent's lead on play of the hand. Most likely, you have a lock. For example, if you have 540 and your opponent has 470 going into the last hand, bet 425. If the player hand wins, you win no matter what your opponent has bet. If the player hand loses, you win if your opponent has bet big (360 or more for this example).

Experience shows that on a secret bet on the last hand, generally BR2 will bet big. In theory, you should use a mixed strategy of maybe betting small, maybe betting big, and maybe betting someplace in the middle. If your opponent is a tournament expert, you might consider using a mixed strategy.

If your opponent's bankroll is less than the maximum bet, do not double down or split on the last hand. If your opponent has bet as big as you expect, s/he does not have enough chips left to split. Even if your opponent has a few chips left and so can double for less, you should have bet enough to win without doubling down yourself.

If you play first you should hope your opponent does double down, because then you can stand on your three-card hand no matter what it is, and be certain that you are matching your opponent's play of the cards. For example, using the numbers of the above example, suppose you have 540, your opponent has 470, you make a secret bet of 425, and your opponent makes a secret bet. Now suppose the player hand gets nine and the dealer shows a 5. Suppose you hit, and your opponent doubles down. The next card is a 2, so now the player hand is eleven. What play do you make? You should stand, of course. In doubling down, your opponent most likely has gone all in; and by standing on the same cards your opponent stands on, you have a lock. If you were to hit the eleven, you could lose or push while your opponent wins. (Your hit card would be the dealer's hit card for your opponent.)

Another example — and this really happened to me. I had a lead of 700 to 400 going into the last hand. My opponent and I both made secret bets; my secret bet was 210. The player hand was eighteen, and the dealer showed 10. My opponent doubled down! On hard eighteen! What was my best play? If I stood on the hard eighteen, I could have lost or pushed the hand while my opponent won, and this could cost me the match if my opponent bet big enough. If I doubled down on hard eighteen and lost, I could lose the match if my opponent bet small enough. If I took the same number of cards that my opponent took, I defeated him no matter whether the player hand won or lost. Thus my best play was to hit the hard eighteen. (The hit card was a 3, and the dealer had 8 in the hole. Thus doubling down on hard eighteen won, while standing would have pushed. My opponent had bet the minimum.)

You Are Behind

You do not want to be behind going into the final bet; but if you are behind, make a secret bet if they are offered. Use a mixed strategy of maybe the minimum, maybe the maximum, and maybe something in the middle. Your opponent has a lock if s/he has managed to match your bet, but do not worry about it because no matter what you bet, there is a range of bets your opponent could make that would effectively match your bet.

If you play second and you are behind, and the playing decision is reasonably close, stand if your opponent hits and hit if your opponent stands.

SECTION B

CRAPS

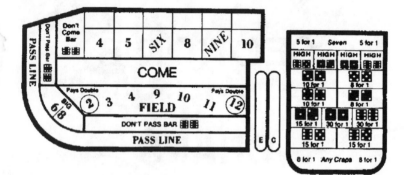

CHAPTER 10

INTRODUCTION

TO TOURNAMENT

CRAPS

This section of the book explains how to play crap tournaments. Chapters 11 through 15 originally were published in 1987 as *Tournament Craps*. Chapter 11 explains the basics of playing tournament craps, and also explains the various bets available at craps. Chapter 12 explains what to bet during the tournament from the first bet up until the final ten minutes or ten rolls of the dice. Chapter 13 explains the end game for sessions that end when the final shooter sevens out. Chapter 14 explains the end game for sessions that end on a particular roll of the dice that is identified in advance. Chapter 15 is miscellaneous comments on playing crap tournaments. Chapter 16 is other material on craps that has little or nothing to do with tournaments.

Most of what I know about playing crap tournaments I have learned from watching others. I take credit for compiling and publishing this material, but I do not claim to be the first to have discovered it. There were experts at tournament craps years before I played my first tournament. I learned from competing against them.

Mostly I learned from losing. I paid my entry fees, the experts beat me out of the prize money, and I learned. When I lost because an opponent made a good play, I analyzed the play and made it part of my own arsenal. When I lost because I made a mistake, I set up a playing procedure that would help me avoid making the same mistake in the future. (I do not mind making a mistake, but I hate to make the same mistake twice.) Thus I developed this material by playing and watching tournaments and then figuring out what happened in a particular situation and why.

CHAPTER 11
THE BASICS OF
TOURNAMENT
CRAPS

This chapter is an introduction to craps and covers the basics of tournament craps. It explains the various bets available at a crap table.

Overview of Betting Strategy

Most of your edge in crap tournaments comes from a simple money-management strategy: Either win or bust out. Seldom should a tournament expert lose with chips left.

The details of proper betting strategy depend on how many people per table advance to the next round, how many good players are at the table, how the end of the round is determined, and the size of maximum bets in relation to your bankroll. These details are explained starting in chapter 12.

Definitions

BR1

If you have not read chapter 1, go back and read it now. You need to know what is meant by BR1, BR2, and so forth.

Most Serious Opponent

Your most serious opponent is the person who is most likely to beat you if you ignore that person. When you are BR*, your most serious opponent generally is the person with the highest bankroll that is not BR*. However, an opponent with $400 who is willing to make big bets is more likely to beat you than someone who has $500 but will never make a big bet. And of course some of your opponents you may recognize as having played skillfully in past tournaments. So your most serious opponent is the person who has the best combination of bankroll and either tournament skills or aggressiveness.

Chip Counting: The Critical Skill

The most important skill required to win prizes in crap tournaments is being able to tell how many chips your opponents have. You have a big edge in a crap tournament if you can tell precisely how you stand compared to your competition.

Of course you have to be able to estimate fairly precisely how many chips your opponents have in the rack in front of them. That is not easy. It is easy to underestimate the bankroll of an opponent on the other end of the table. The more chips someone has the harder it is to estimate the bankroll. Practicing chip counting is a good idea.

For someone who has a monster pile of chips, you might try estimating inches of chips rather than number of chips.

Watch your opponents' hands. Competitors are not allowed to have tournament chips in their hands except temporarily while making a bet or removing chips from the layout. Chips not currently being bet belong in the rack, not in the hand. Anytime you see an opponent holding chips in a hand, you should immediately ask a supervisor to correct the situation. Likewise you should complain if an opponent's chips are in the rack but covered by hands or arms or whatever. If you are beaten, be sure it is because of luck or skill; do not get beaten by hidden chips.

You also need to know how many additional chips your opponents will have if the next roll of the dice is a 7. Bets that win on a 7 are: don't pass after a point is established, don't come bets that have been moved behind the numbers, buy bets behind the numbers, last come bets, proposition bets on 7, and hop bets on 1-6, 2-5, and 3-4. (If you do not understand these terms, read on. They will be explained by the end of this chapter.)

For example, suppose you have $750 in the rack, two people have more chips in the rack than you do, and you want to be in the top three. Are you BR3? Maybe, and maybe not. If the point is 4 and someone has $100 on the don't pass with $400 odds on it, that person will add $800 to the rack if a 7 rolls. That person might have zero in the rack right now, but you cannot sit on your $750 because if a 7 rolls you are BR4. You do not have the position you want, so you have to make a bet.

Undercounting an opponent's chips seems to be much more common than overcounting them, and is more costly. So play it safe. If more than two people advance from your table, do not try to be BRN, the lowest bankroll of those that advance; it is safer to try to be the next higher bankroll. For example, if six people will advance from your table, try to be BR5 or higher.

Should You Shoot the Dice?

Craps is played with two dice that are rolled by a customer called the "shooter." The shooter keeps the dice for a "hand" (explained later), after which the dice pass clockwise to the next shooter. Generally you have the right to pass the dice, meaning you do not have to be the shooter. In a regular crap game, there is no advantage or disadvantage associated with being the shooter.

In a tournament it generally does not matter whether you shoot the dice. An exception is that in some tournaments, on the last roll or last few rolls the bets must be placed in order, moving clockwise around the table starting with the bettor to the left of the shooter. It definitely is to your advantage to be among the last to bet on the final rolls. Tournaments with a bet-in-order rule generally do not allow a competitor to pass the dice. But if you are going to have to bet in order on the final roll or rolls, and if you have the option of passing the dice, then pass if you think it will give you a better shooting order for the end game.

Some tournaments are for a predetermined amount of time, some are for a predetermined number of rolls of the dice, and some are a mixture of the two. For tournaments based on time, you should like to shoot the dice because you can be quick and thus get in as many rolls per minute as possible. You do not do this just so the house edge has a better chance of grinding down those of your opponents who are making high-house-percentage bets such as proposition bets; you also do it to cut down on the amount of time your opponents have for thinking.

In one tournament I had about $1400 and one of the people I had to stay ahead of had about $1200. I was the final shooter. My opponent kept saying "I think I should make a bet," but every time the stickman gave me the dice I threw them right away. My opponent never did make a bet.

Bets at Craps

The rest of this chapter explains the various bets that can be made at craps.

Pass Line

Every contestant is required to have a bet in action at all times. Most tournaments require a pass or don't pass bet, but other tournaments allow a bet anywhere on the layout.

The most common bets made on the crap table are on the pass line. The appropriate time to bet the pass line is when the shooter is "coming out for a point." In other words, no point is yet established. ("Point" is explained in the following paragraph.) If the first roll of the dice is 7 or 11, that roll is called a "pass" and pass-line bets win. If the first roll of the dice is 2, 3, or 12 (which are called crap rolls), pass-line bets lose.

If the first roll of the dice is 4, 5, 6, 8, 9, or 10, that number is called the point. Once a point is established, all pass-line bets are locked in place for roll after roll of the dice until either the point or a 7 is rolled. Sometimes the dice roll many times before the fate of the pass line is decided. If the point number rolls again before a 7 rolls, pass-line bets win; this also is called a pass. If a 7 rolls before the point is rolled, the pass line loses, the hand is over, and the dice go to the next shooter.

The casino has about 1.4% edge on pass-line bets. The average pass-line bet is decided in 3.376 rolls, making the casino edge effectively 0.41% per roll. At 120 to 180 rolls per hour, the overall player loss rate is half to three-quarters of a pass or don't-pass bet per hour.

Pass-line bets have no flexibility. Once a point is established, you cannot reduce your pass-line bet. It is stuck until either the point is rolled or a 7 is rolled. You can increase your pass-line bet if you want to, but there probably is no reason why you would want to.

Odds on Pass-Line Bets

Once a point is established, you can take "odds" on your pass-line bet. The casino specifies a maximum on the amount of your odds bet; generally you are allowed up to double your pass-line bet.

Odds is a free bet in the sense that the casino takes no percentage on it. Out of the 36 possible rolls of the dice, there are three ways to roll 4, four ways to roll 5, five ways to roll 6, six ways to roll 7, five ways to roll 8, four ways to roll 9, and three ways to roll 10. Those numbers of ways determine the payoffs on odds. If the point is 4 or 10, your odds bet wins double if the point is rolled before a 7; you have three ways to make your point and six ways to lose, so the double payoff gives the casino no edge. If the point is 5 or 9, your odds bet wins three to two. If the point is 6 or 8, your odds bet wins six to five.

Sometimes a casino allows more than double odds even though the tournament's rules specify a maximum of double odds. For a point of six or eight, commonly you can put up two and a half times your bet to win three times your bet. At some casinos, with a three-chip bet you can take ten chips of odds no matter what the point. Since there is no general rule on the maximum for odds bets, even if the written rules say "double odds," you should ask about the details at the rules meeting if nobody else asks first.

Odds bets are flexible; you can make them or remove them as you want.

Don't Pass

This bet is almost exactly the opposite of the pass line. The exception is that if the first roll of the dice is 12 (some casinos use 2 instead of 12), pass-line bets lose and don't pass bets have a standoff. Thus if you bet a dollar on both the pass line and the don't pass, 35/36 of the time one of your bets will lose and the other will win. The other 1/36 of the time, your pass-line bet will lose and your don't pass bet will not win.

The casino's edge on the don't pass is about 1.4%. (The casino has a tiny bit less of an edge on don't pass than on pass-line bets.)

Don't pass bets are flexible. You can remove them anytime you want. The reason the casino is willing to let you remove them is you are giving up a percentage by removing a don't pass bet after a point is established. Suppose you have $10 on the don't pass and the point is

6. You have six ways to win that bet and only five ways to lose it. The expected value of that bet is $10.91. That is, $10 on the don't pass with a point of 6 will sometimes turn into $20 and sometimes turn into zero, but on average will turn into $10.91. So the casino is happy if you want to settle for just $10. Don't pass bets are flexible, but removing a don't pass bet means giving the casino more than its usual 1.4%.

You also can make an odds bet on your don't pass bet. This is called "laying odds," whereas on a pass-line bet it is called "taking odds." The payoffs are the reverse of those for pass-line odds. If the point is 4 or 10, you win half on your odds bet. As an example, suppose you have $10 bet on the don't pass and the casino allows double odds; if the point is 4 you can lay $40 to win $20 that a 7 will roll before a 4. If the point is 5 or 9 you can lay $30 to win $20. If the point is 6 or 8 you can lay $24 to win $20. Odds bets are flexible; you can make them or pick them up at any time.

Come

Come bets are similar to pass-line bets. If the next roll of the dice is 7 or 11, the come bet wins. If the next roll of the dice is 2, 3, or 12, the come bet loses. If the next roll of the dice is any other number, the dealer picks up the come bet and moves it to a part of the layout containing the number that just rolled. If that number is rolled again before a 7, that come bet wins. If a 7 comes first, that come bet loses. The main difference between the come bet and the pass-line bet is the dealer picks up the come bet and moves it after a number rolls.

You can take odds on come bets the same as you take odds on pass-line bets. You must give your odds to the dealer to place on top of or next to the come bet.

The casino's edge on come bets is the same 1.4% as on pass-line bets. Come bets are as inflexible as pass-line bets.

Don't Come

Don't come bets are to don't pass as come bets are to pass-line bets. If the next roll of the dice is 2, or 3, the don't come bet wins; if the next roll is 7 or 11, the don't come bet loses. If any other number is rolled, the dealer picks up the don't come bet and places it behind the appropriate number. Thereafter, if a 7 rolls the don't come bet wins, and if the number rolls again the don't come bet loses.

Don't bettors are sometimes called "wrong" bettors, as opposed to "right" bettors who bet the pass line, the come, and make place bets. There is nothing wrong with betting "wrong," particularly in a tournament.

Odds can be laid on the don't come bet.

House edge and flexibility are the same as for don't pass.

Place Bets

You place a number by setting chips on a neutral place on the table and telling the dealer what you want. You can place the 6 or 8 by putting up $6 to win $7. That is, if you place the 6 for $6 you lose that bet if a 7 rolls but if a 6 rolls you win $7.

On place bets on 6 and 8, the house edge is 1.5%. The average place bet on 6 or 8 is decided in 3.273 rolls, making the effective casino edge 0.46%. Thus place bets on 6 and 8 are only slightly more costly than pass and don't pass bets.

You can place the 5 or 9 by putting up $5 to win $7. The house edge on those bets is 4%.

In some casinos you can place the 4 and 10, putting up $5 to win $9. The casino edge on those bets is 6.7%. Some casinos do not allow place bets on 4 and 10.

Place bets have the advantage of complete flexibility. You can put them up or remove them at will.

Buy Bets

You can buy a number by giving the casino a 5% commission on the payoff. For example, you can buy the 4 by giving the dealer $100 to win $200, and tossing in another $5 for the commission. If you win you are ahead $195, and if you lose you are out $105. Buying the 4 and 10 has a lower casino edge (5%) than placing them, and that is why people who want to bet the 4 or 10 buy the number instead of placing it.

Some casinos allow both buy and place bets on every number. You buy the 5 or 9 by giving the dealer $100 to win $150 and also giving the dealer $5 commission. You buy the 6 or 8 by giving the dealer $100 to win $120 and also giving the dealer $5 commission.

Most common is to allow either buy bets or place bets but not both. Therefore, if you want to bet on 4 and 10 you do it with buy bets, and if you want to bet on 5, 6, 8, or 9 you place them. If both place and buy bets are allowed on all the numbers, you must understand this book to say "both place and buy" where it says just "place" or just "buy."

Buy bets, like place bets, have complete flexibility. You can put them up or take them down at will. If you take down a buy bet, the commission is returned to you.

How to Make Place and Buy Bets

There is an established procedure for making place bets and buy bets. First, set your chips on the felt in a place where they cannot be construed as being a bet. For example, you may set them down straddling a line. Second, tell the dealer what to do with your chips. The dealer will reach for the chips while listening to your explanation of how you want to bet them. You will have action on your bets even if the dealer does not get your chips arranged properly on the layout before the dice roll.

It is important to do this right in a tournament. You want to control when and how much you bet; if you end up with a bet different from what you want, that is your fault and not the dealer's.

Removing Place and Buy Bets

To remove your place and buy bets, ask the dealer to take your bets "down." The dealer will pick up your chips and set them on the felt in front of you. Frequently a customer will remove only one or a few place bets and leave the others working; so if you want to remove all of yours, watch to be sure the dealer gets them all. If one or two of your bets accidentally are not removed, they have action when the dice roll.

You also can ask that your bets be "off," which means they stay on the layout but have no action on the next roll. The dealer will place a small disk on the top of each bet that is off. You can take bets off for one roll or for roll after roll until you ask that they be "on."

The difference between bets down and bets off is when you take the bets down you put the chips in the rack, and when your bets are off the chips stay on the layout.

Big 6 and Big 8

These are bets that the number will roll before a 7. A bet on the big 6 wins even money if a 6 rolls and loses if a 7 rolls. These bets give the casino 9.1%, so knowledgeable crapshooters would rather make place bets. Big 6 and big 8 bets have complete flexibility; you can make or remove them at will. At most casinos you can bet the big 6 and big 8 even if you have already placed those numbers for the maximum.

Buying Behind the Numbers

You can bet that a 7 will roll before a particular number. You do this by giving your bet to the dealer plus a 5% commission on the payoff. You get the true odds on your bet (except for the commission). For example, you can give the dealer $200 to put behind the 10 to win $100 if a 7 rolls before a 10. You also give the dealer $5 commission. Thus you either win a net of $95 or lose $205. Other names for this bet are "betting the 10 to lose" and "$200 no 10."

You buy behind the 4 and 10 by putting up $200 to win $100, plus you pay the dealer a $5 commission. You buy behind the 5 and 9 with $150 to win $100 plus you pay the dealer a $5 commission. You buy behind the 6 and

8 with $120 to win $100 plus you give the dealer a 5% commission.

Buying behind numbers has complete flexibility. If you take these bets down the commission is returned to you.

Placing to Lose

Some books on how to play craps mention "placing to lose" as being the opposite of a place bet, just like buying behind a number is the opposite of buying the number. However, I have yet to find a casino that would allow me to place a number to lose.

Field

A field bets wins if the next roll of the dice is 2, 3, 4, 9, 10, 11, or 12. If the next roll is 5, 6, 7, or 8, the field bet loses. In some casinos 2 and 12 both pay double in the field; in other casinos, one of those numbers pays double and the other pays triple. If both pay double, the casino edge on field bets is 5.6%; if one pays double and the other pays triple, the casino edge is 2.8%.

The field bet is a one-roll bet; the next roll of the dice will decide the field bet for certain. And you have complete flexibility with field bets; you can make them or remove them as is your pleasure.

Propositions

Other bets are called proposition bets. Most of them give the casino a fairly healthy percentage, which is why the dealers sometimes hustle the customers to make them. The payouts, and thus the casino's edge, vary from casino to casino. You can bet that the next roll of the dice is 2. Or 3. Or 11. Or 12.

Or you can bet on any other two-dice combination. This is called a hop bet. If you toss a chip onto the layout and say "4-3 on the hop," you will win the same as the payoff on 11 — fourteen or fifteen times your bet — if the next roll of the dice is 4-3, and you will lose your bet if the next roll is not 4-3. If you bet a pair on the hop, such as 4-4, the payoff is the same as if you win a bet on 12.

Or you can bet on any craps; or any 7.

Or you can bet the hard ways. A bet on hard 8 is an example. If 4-4 rolls, this bet wins. If 2-6, 3-5, or any 7 rolls, this bet loses.

What Bets to Make and When

The next three chapters explain which of these bets to use and when you use them. Chapter 12 goes from your first bet up until the final ten minutes or ten rolls. Chapters 13 and 14 cover the final bets for the two different formats used to end sessions of crap tournaments.

CHAPTER 12
THE EARLY AND
MIDDLE GAME

This chapter explains your first bet and all subsequent bets up until the final ten minutes or ten rolls of the dice. It explains when to make a move to become BR*, how to make a move to become BR*, and how to attempt to stay BR*.

First Bet

Initially you want to conserve your chips. There is a chance that preserving your starting bankroll will allow you to advance to the next round. This is particularly true if several people from your table will be advancing to the next round. If six advance from your table, for example, play very conservatively and start out betting the minimum required.

In craps, every bet you make has a negative expectation except for odds, which has a zero expectation. You are at a disadvantage no matter what bet you make. However, this is not the reason you start out with a minimum bet; you start out with a minimum bet because of all the bets that might enable you to advance to the next round, a minimum bet give you the best combination of likelihood of advancing if you win and likelihood of advancing if you lose.

Generally you start with a minimum bet on the pass or don't pass. Which of those you bet does not matter.

Subsequent Bets

Early on you do not know who your most serious opponents will turn out to be. All of your opponents have large enough bankrolls to be threats to you, so you have to play against all of them. Try to monitor your bankroll position continuously. That is, try to always have a good idea of whether you are BR1, BR2, etc. And always keep in mind how many people are going to advance to the next round. Keep track of which players have the largest bankrolls and notice what bets they make.

If You Are BR* in the Early Going

The important thing is to give yourself a chance to stay BR*. You may not be able to guarantee that you will still be BR* after the dice roll, but at least you want there to be some rolls that would keep you in the BR* spot.

Generally most of your opponents bet small in the early going. When that happens, stick with minimum bets.

Sometimes, however, most of your opponents make bets larger than the minimum, and they all bet "right." They make come bets and place bets and take odds. When that happens you should make small place bets and take odds on your pass-line bet. You should generally avoid come bets because of their lack of flexibility. If the bankrolls of your opponents drift upward, your bankroll will drift up too, but not as much. If your opponents lose, you do not mind losing as long as you lose less than they do.

While it is best to make minimum bets as BR* in the early going, if you want to make bets larger than the minimum or make bets in addition to the minimum required, go ahead but keep the bets small and try to bet the same way (i.e. right or wrong) as your most serious opponents are betting.

If You Are Not BR* in the Early Going

What you should do if you are not BR* depends on how you size up your opponents. For example, often an opponent will bet wildly, get considerably ahead of you, and continue betting wildly. Smile when you have an opponent like that, because generally (but not every time) that opponent will continue to bet wildly and finally bust out. You do not have to go get that opponent; just wait and s/he comes back to you.

If most of the money being bet is bet one way, bet the other way. For example, frequently most of your opponents bet the pass line, bet the come, and make place bets; little money is bet on the don't pass and don't come. If such is the case and you are not BR*, bet the don't pass.

After you are able to identify particular opponents as the people you need to catch, try to bet opposite to the way they are betting. Try to bet opposite the most dollars, not the most bets. For example, with three people ahead of you and one betting $100 on the pass line and the other two betting $10 on the don't pass, bet the don't pass.

You can make more than minimum bets. If you are not BR*, you can use a fluctuation in your bankroll. You want to win of course, but to take a chance on winning you have to take a chance on losing. For example, you might take or lay odds if you are not BR*.

If you want to play craps during the crap tournament, this is the time to do it. That is, if you want to bet hardways or the field or whatever sometime during the play of the tournament, the only appropriate spot is in the early going when you are not BR*. Try to make bets different from those of the people you are trying to catch, to give yourself a chance to catch them.

When to Make a Major Move to Become BR*

Many times people advance in a crap tournament without having to make a big bet. This happens more often when your opponents are crapshooters rather than experienced tournament players. Most crapshooters seem to bet "right;" that is, they bet the pass line and make come bets and take odds. They make place bets and bet the hardways. They bet on 11 and any craps. The reason this helps you in a tournament is if all of your opponents bet the same way, either they all lose or they all win. If the dice are cold, all of their bankrolls go down quickly while yours goes down slowly; at the end of the session your opponents either are gone or do not know how to threaten you with the few chips they have left. If the dice are hot and your opponents all win, you know how to threaten the leaders with the chips you have left.

As soon as you realize that your present bankroll will not be enough to allow you to advance to the next round, make a big bet in an attempt to get the bankroll position you want. Here are the factors to consider.

Number of Good Tournament Players

If there are more good tournament players at your table than the number of players that will be advancing to the next round, most likely an amount greater than your starting bankroll will be required to advance. In that situation, you can make a major move early in an attempt to become BR*.

Number of Winners Per Table

The fewer winners per table, the earlier you should try to become BR*. If only two people advance to the next round, you probably should start out with a minimum bet but would be none the worse for starting out with a higher bet.

With one winner per table, or on the final table where the winner gets a prize that is considerably larger than second prize, keep yourself in contention for the BR1 spot right from the start. You might even consider going all-in on the first roll of the dice. If someone gets ahead of you, immediately attempt to regain the lead.

Example

Here is an example explaining exactly when I decided to make a major move. In a Four Queens crap tournament, two people were going to advance to the next round out of ten of us. We each bought in for $500. One player started with $100 on the don't pass, took full double odds, and won $300 when the first shooter sevened out. Then he dropped to $25 bets. About ten minutes later another player won a series of place bets and ran his bankroll up to about $800, after which he switched to minimum $5 bets. I was BR3 with $545. The other seven players all were betting small and all had $500 plus or minus a little. With two players between $250 and $300 ahead of me and seven other players right behind me and everybody betting small, I decided that $545 would not be enough to advance to the next round. So I made a major move to become BR*.

Low Max Games

A low-max game is one in which the max bet is low compared to the bankrolls. An extreme example is a tournament in which each player starts out with 100,000 in chips but the maximum bet is 10,000. In a low-max game, if there is but one winner per table it is a certainty that your initial bankroll will not win the table. In that situation, make big bets from the start. Many of your opponents will be betting big; some will bet big on the numbers, and others will bet big behind the numbers. If you bet small to start, some of your opponents will be way ahead of you for certain, and it will be very difficult for you to get the BR1 spot. You may find yourself locked out; that is, you may have plenty of chips but no way to bet them that can win the tournament because every bet you consider is already being made by someone with more chips than you.

How To Make a Major Move to Become BR*

Once you have decided to make a major move, you want to maximize your chance of success. Maximizing your chance of becoming BR* generally means betting as many of your chips as possible, and, unfortunately, usually means taking a chance of busting out. Bet all your chips if you can, and bet them all in a coordinated manner.

When you make a major move, you want to either become BR* or bust out; you do not want any other result. If you lose you want to lose all your chips, not just part of them.

The only time to bet less than all your chips in a major move to catch up is when the maximum is so low that you cannot bet the rest of your chips the way you want to bet them.

Place Bets

When you go all in, a good way to do it is on place bets. In the Four Queens example above, where I decided to make a major move with my $545 to catch two players who had about $800, I placed the 6 and 8 for $270 each. Since I also had $5 on the pass line, I was all-in. A 7 would have wiped me out. But I caught a 6, won $315 to become BR1, and took down my place bets.

Place the 6 and 8 for as much as you can. If you have money left over after placing them for the max, place the 5. If you still have money left over, place the 9. If you still have money left, buy the 4. If you still have money left, buy the 10. If you are required to make a bet on pass or don't pass, bet on pass. You also can take odds on your pass-line bet. And you can bet the big 6 and big 8.

The most efficient time to make your big place bets is when the shooter already has a point, because then a 7 will wipe you out completely. But if the people you are trying to catch are making big place bets but not on the come-out roll, then have place bets working on the come-out roll to get the swing you need.

If you win a big bet and are still short of your target, parlay your winnings and keep betting your whole bankroll until it is the size you need.

4, 9, 10, Field

An alternative, when the person you are trying to catch is complicating your task by placing the 6 and 8 big, is to place or buy the 4, 9, and 10 with large bets, and make a large field bet. If a 4, 9, or 10 rolls, you win more than someone who has merely made the large place bets but no field bet. If a 7 rolls you lose all four of your large bets, but the person ahead of you who has gone up big on all the numbers could lose six large bets and drop behind you.

The way to make these large bets, if the person you are trying to catch is watching you carefully with the intent of matching your bets, is to go up with bets on the 4, 9, and 10 first. Then when your opponent transfers attention to the dealer to make matching place bets on the 4, 9, and 10, you quietly make your field bet.

5, 6, 8, Field

Another strategy, for use when an opponent is trying to match your bets, is to bet approximately a fourth of your bankroll as place bets on each of 5, 6, and 8. Then when your opponent is making bets and paying less attention to you, quietly bet the rest of your money in the field. If your opponent does not see your field bet, you will catch up if the next roll of the dice is a field roll. Of course that opponent will be even farther ahead of you if a 5, 6, or 8 rolls, and you will be wiped out if a 7 rolls. But you do have 16/36 chance of winning a field bet.

A variation on this is to make big bets on the 6, 8, and field. Put about a third of your bankroll as place bets on 6 and 8. Then when your opponent turns to the dealer to place the 6 and 8, put the rest of your bankroll in the field.

Betting Behind a Number

If the people you are trying to catch have their money up as place bets or come bets on the numbers ("betting right" in crap parlance), then your best chance of getting the swing you need is to buy behind a number. If the maximum is large enough, buy behind one of the numbers with all of your money. It is better to have all of your money riding behind one number rather than split up behind several numbers, so that if you lose you lose it all at once.

Of course if you have so much money that you have to bet behind several numbers, then that is what you do.

Sometimes the person you are trying to catch has such a large bet riding on a number that you can get the swing you need with a bet behind just that one number. For example, suppose that in a tournament with a $300 maximum bet, BR1 has $300 on the pass line, the point is 10, and BR1 takes $600 odds. You can lay $600 to win $300 behind the 10, and if a 7 rolls you win $285 while BR1 loses $900 for a $1185 swing.

If the maximum is too small for you to bet all of your money as a buy bet behind one number, you still may be able to get all of your money in action behind a number by way of the don't pass or don't come. If double odds are allowed, bet at least 25% (30% with exact double odds) of your bankroll on the don't pass (or don't come) and after the shooter has a point, lay odds with the rest of your money.

If your bankroll is too big for you to get the whole thing in action behind one number via the don't pass or don't come, you can combine that bet with buying behind the same number. For example, if your bankroll is more than four times the maximum bet, you may not be able to bet your whole bankroll on the don't pass or don't come, even with double odds. But you can bet the maximum on the don't pass (or don't come), and as soon as your bet is behind a number, lay as much odds as you can. In addition, buy behind the same number.

For example, suppose the maximum bet is $300 and exact double odds are allowed. If you bet $300 on the don't pass and the point is 6 or 8, you can lay $720 odds to win $600. And you can buy behind the point for $360 to win $300, giving the casino $15 commission. In total you have risked $1395. If the shooter makes the point, you lose the whole $1395. If the shooter sevens out, you win $1185. If the point is 5 or 9, you can risk as much as $1665 to win $1185. If the point is 4 or 10, you can risk as much as $2115 to win $1185.

If the person you are trying to catch is a skillful tournament player, the best way for you to catch up is to make a large bet on don't pass or don't come. After your bet is behind a number, lay as much odds as you can. And then bet the rest of your money behind the same number. If that number rolls, you are wiped out; if a 7 rolls, you win. Generally when you go up behind a number with all your bankroll, the person you are trying to catch will not correlate with you; whereas if you went up on place bets instead, a good tournament player would make bets to correlate with you.

Correlating to Stay BR*

When you are BR*, decide which of your opponents is the most serious threat. Once you have identified that person, try to correlate your bets with that person's bets. That is, bet the same way the most serious threat is betting, but smaller amounts. Your goals are if the most serious threat wins a bet you want to stay ahead of him or her, and if that person loses a bet you want to have enough chips left to still be BR*.

If two opponents are equally serious threats, pick out one to correlate with. This is particularly true if they bet opposite from each other; correlate with one and let the other one have a shot at catching you. You have no better alternative. The only alternative is to correlate with neither and let both have a shot at you, which will result in one of them passing you.

Sometimes a person other than the one with which you have decided to correlate wins enough to get ahead of you. And sometimes the person with whom you are trying to correlate manages to get ahead of you. In either case, when you find you no longer are BR*, go all in to attempt to regain the BR* spot.

Waiting For the Last Few Minutes to Become BR*

You cannot wait for the last five or ten minutes (or five or ten rolls) to get the BR* spot, for three reasons.

First, if you are behind you are forced to bet first; if you try to wait for your opponents to bet first, they will not bet and the stick man will call "No more bets."

Second, you have almost no time to analyze the situation, and with everyone's bankrolls fluctuating wildly you may not be able to come up with the bets that give you the best chance of catching up. Betting while ahead is easier to do with limited thinking time, since it means simply matching someone else's bets.

Third, toward the end everyone tends to bet big, and if you are not BR* you may find yourself locked out;

no matter where you put your money, enough people ahead of you in bankrolls may also be making the same bets so that you do not have a chance. A major move is only effective if the people you are trying to catch are not making the same bets that you are making.

CHAPTER 13 END GAME: LAST SHOOTER SEVENS OUT

This chapter covers the end game for sessions that end when the last shooter sevens out. It covers the last five or ten minutes, or five or ten rolls, before the last shooter is identified; it also covers bets made while the final shooter is rolling.

Last Five or Ten Minutes Before Last Shooter Identified

At this point you should be BR*. You should have been either making small bets or correlating with your most serious competitor. If you are not BR* you should immediately risk all of your bankroll in an effort to become BR*.

Correlating to Stay BR*

Match the bets of your most serious opponent more closely than you had been doing earlier. Bet enough so that if your most serious opponent wins a bet, you stay ahead of him or her. If you have to make max bets to do that, make max bets.

An Alternative: Laying the Point

Correlating makes the most sense when you can stay BR* whether you win or lose, or when you have but one serious competitor. Sometimes you have multiple serious competitors and they are betting so heavily on the numbers that you must go virtually all-in if you want to correlate with them. If you do correlate with them and catch a 7, you will lose so much that others of your competitors will be ahead of you. If you cannot correlate with small enough place bets to stay BR* if a 7 rolls, then consider buying behind a number with a max bet.

The reason for making this bet is if you do not make big place bets, you need a 7 to keep your lead — if numbers roll, you will no longer be BR*. Since you need a 7 anyway, you might as well make a bet that gives you a few more chips if a 7 rolls.

The number to bet behind is the number that is being bet most heavily by your most serious opponents. Usually it is the point.

Here is an example. Two people advance, the maximum bet is $300, BR1 has $2000, and you are BR2 with $1500. Several others of your opponents have over $1200, have large pass-line bets with odds, and are making large come bets and place bets. Others of your opponents are still sitting on their $500 buy-ins. BR1 has

$300 on the line and $600 odds. The point is 10. This is a good time to buy behind the 10 with $600 to win $300.

When You Are Not BR*

If you drop out of the BR* spot, you should immediately bet in a manner that gives you a chance to regain the BR* spot. This probably means going all-in on place bets; but it might mean making a max bet behind one number, or going all-in behind as many numbers as are required, or betting the 4, 9, 10, and field. This list is not all-inclusive. Whatever bets give you a chance, you make. One thing you should not do at this late stage is keep your chips in the rack if you are not BR*.

Betting in Order

If the contestants are betting in order, keep track of the time. If the final shooter will be announced in less than two minutes and you are not the last bettor, when your turn to bet comes you should bet as if the present shooter is the last shooter. You make your bets and then are locked in until after the dice roll once more. If the last shooter is announced before your opponents finish making their bets and before the dice roll again, this shooter is the last shooter but you will not be able to change your bets until after the dice roll once more. I once was caught with inappropriate bets out and fortunately the 7 did not roll. You can learn from my experience — do not let that happen to you.

Bets While Final Shooter Is Rolling

This section covers bets after the final shooter is identified. The session could be over in one more roll of the dice or the final shooter could hold the dice for an hour. I have seen both.

Make sure you are BR*. In figuring whether you are BR*, you have to consider bets made by your opponents that will win if a 7 rolls. This means don't pass bets and odds on them, come bets, don't come bets that have gone behind numbers and odds on those bets, buy bets behind numbers, bets on any 7, and hop bets on 1-6, 2-5, and 3-4. It is not enough to be BR* in terms of chips in the rack; you have to be BR* if the next roll of the dice is 7.

Bets As BR*

What you should do depends on what your opponents do. If you can make bets that give you a lock, do it. This situation arises if all the people who are not BR* are betting the same way. This happens frequently when your opponents are all crapshooters rather than experienced tournament players; they all bet the pass line and make come bets and place numbers. If you can approximately match their bets to guarantee you will stay ahead of them, do it.

Here is an situation that really happened to me. One person was going to advance to the next round. The point was 10 when the final shooter was announced. I was BR1 with $750. BR2 had $600 in the rack and $20 on the pass line, and was placing the 6 and 8 for $30 each. BR3 had $620 in the rack and was betting $50 on the don't pass. I had $50 on the don't pass, placed the 6 and 8 for $30 each, and kept my other $640 in the rack. We kept these same bets for half a dozen rolls of the dice before a 7 finally came and made me the winner.

Locks do occur, and frequently. They are most common when several people advance to the next round. For example, one time everybody busted out at my table except for four of us, and three of us were going to go on to the next round. I matched BR4 bet for bet for the last shooter's hand. When BR4 bet $10 on hard 8, I bet $10 on hard 8. There was no way that BR4 could possibly have gotten ahead of me as long as I was able to match his bets.

If you are BR* and this is the last shooter, and you are matching your most serious opponent bet for bet, be alert because that person should try to sneak in a quick bet just before the stick man calls "No more bets."

If you can identify some of your chips as being excess, use them for place bets. For example, suppose you have $1100 and your most serious competitor who is not BR* has 800. You do not need all $1100 to stay BR*; $801 will do. You can afford to make place bets with up to $299 of your bankroll. Consider placing the 6 and 8 for $120 each. This gives you a better chance of advancing to the next round in the event the final hand is a long one.

Bets If You Are Not BR*

If you are not BR*, or if you are in doubt as to whether you are BR*, do something about it. One possibility is bets behind the numbers (if allowed; some casinos does not allow them in their tournaments). If you can bet enough behind the point so that a 7 on the next roll will make you BR*, do it. If going behind the point will not win enough but going up behind another number or more numbers will make you BR* if a 7 rolls, make those bets. Going up behind 6 and 8 wins more for a given bet size; 5 and 9 are next best, and then come 4 and 10.

The important thing with bets behind the numbers is to reassess the situation after every roll of the dice. If a number rolls and either your opponents win money or one of your bets loses, you have got to refigure whether you will be BR* if the next roll is a 7. If you do not think you will be BR* if the next roll is a 7, then you have got to immediately take down your bets from behind the numbers and replace them with bets that give you a chance.

If bets behind the numbers are not allowed, or if they would not win you enough to be BR*, then bet your whole bankroll as place bets. You may have to be all-in on place bets for several rolls of the dice before you can take them down and hope a 7 ends the session while you are BR*.

If too many of the people who are ahead of you are already making max place bets on the numbers you wanted to bet, then bet different numbers. For example, you should prefer to place the 6 and 8; but if winning place bets on those numbers will not make you BR*, then check to see if bets on 5 and 9 will do the job, or bets on 4 and 10. Be willing to make a field bet if that is the only chance you have to get the swing you need.

As you may have guessed, a crap tournament table with more experts than the number of players who will advance to the next round contains a lot of large bets and a lot of moving them around during the final hand. You might be all-in on place bets while an opponent is all-in behind the numbers. When a number rolls and one of your bets wins while one of your opponent's bets loses, you switch to buying behind the numbers and your opponent switches to place bets. Another number rolls and the two of you switch positions again. Whichever of you is lucky enough to be behind the numbers when a 7 rolls will win the table.

Any opponent who has about the same bankroll but keeps those chips in the rack has no way to win.

Betting in Order

If you have to bet in order, you probably must bet all of your chips. If you bet first, keeping your chips in the rack is suicide; your opponents will make bets such that whatever rolls, you will have no chance of advancing to the next round. Either go all-in behind a number or numbers, or go all-in on place bets. If you are BR* you should bet behind a number, and if you are not BR* you should make place bets.

Alternate Ways to End a Session

This chapter has covered the end game for sessions that end when the final shooter sevens out.

Sometimes the last shooter can hold the dice for an hour or more, which causes headaches for the person in charge of scheduling tournament sessions. To relieve that headache, some crap tournaments have sessions that end on a pre-announced roll of the dice. The end game strategy for these tournaments is covered in the next chapter.

In some crap tournaments, at the end of a certain amount of time the remaining players are counted. Then the session ends after whichever occurs first of a seven out or a number of rolls equal to the number of players. If the end of the tournament occurs in this manner, use the advice of this seven-out chapter for all rolls until the last four, at which time you should switch over to the advice of the next chapter.

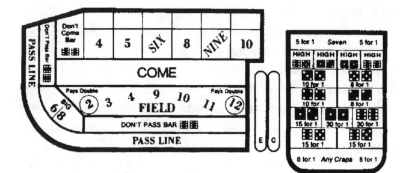

CHAPTER 14
END GAME: FINAL
ROLL KNOWN

This chapter covers the end game for tournaments in which the final roll is identified in advance. The tournament might consist of a set number of rolls of the dice, or it might be a specified time interval plus a set number of rolls. The important feature is that the final roll is known in advance. (If you are playing in a tournament in which the session ends when the final shooter sevens out, you want chapter 13 instead of this chapter.) All players know when the final roll is coming, they make their final bets, and then the dice roll for the final time. After the final winning bets are paid and losing bets are picked up by the dealer, all undecided bets on the layout are returned to the players.

Bets With a Player Edge

You have an 11.1% edge with a final-roll bet on the come. You have 8 ways to win, 4 ways to lose, and 24 ways to push.

Since all unresolved bets are returned after the last roll, come bettors have an edge on the last dozen rolls of the dice, as shown in table 7.

In table 7, "come bet" includes pass-line bets on come-out rolls.

Table 7
Edge on Come Bets
if Final Roll Known

Roll, Counting Backwards	Edge On Come Bet
1	11.1%
2	9.0
3	7.3
4	5.8
5	4.6
6	3.6
7	2.8
8	2.1
9	1.5
10	1.0
11	0.6
12	0.3
13	0.0

Don't-come bettors are at a greater disadvantage than usual, and for the whole session! On the thirteenth roll from the end when come bettors are playing with zero edge, don't-come bettors are playing with a 2.8% disadvantage rather than their normal 1.4% disadvantage.

Unfortunately, the bets you want to make to win your table are not the bets that give you an advantage over the casino.

Though you can make bets that give you an edge over the casino, your expected win on those bets generally is small compared to the prize money at stake in the tournament. Therefore, your first priority is to try to win the tournament, even if you have to pass up bets with a positive expectation. You want all your chips available for betting on the final roll; that means you cannot have any money tied up as come bets locked on numbers, which means you will not be able to take advantage of the positive expectation on come bets on the last dozen rolls.

Bets, Ten Minutes or Ten Rolls Prior to Final Roll

The minimum you want going into the final roll is the bankroll position of BR*. If there is more than one person with enough chips to challenge you, and if you think those people will be willing to bet all their chips on the final roll, then you usually should not be content with being merely BR*; you should like to have a comfortable lead over all competitors who are not BR*. How much of a lead you want depends primarily on your betting position on the final roll. If you will be betting after all of your serious competitors, then any lead is sufficient. If you will have to bet ahead of serious competitors on the final roll, you would like to have a lead over them of at least the maximum on a field bet.

To get the lead you want, make place bets or buy behind one or more numbers. If you need a swing and too many people ahead of you in bankrolls are already loaded up on bets both in front of and behind the numbers, make a field bet.

There are two things that are important here. One is if you are not BR*, you should bet your whole bankroll. Second is you should bet your money with maximum flexibility in mind. Place bets and buy bets give you flexibility; you can change them at will. You would not normally consider a large pass-line or come bet because you cannot change those bets once they go on a number. (In one tournament I did bet $100 on the pass line in such a situation. My table was down to four competitors, and three of us were going to advance to the next round. BR4 bet $100 on the pass line, so I followed with $100 on the pass line. By matching BR4's bet, I had a lock on advancing to the next round of the tournament.)

Bets on the Final Roll

You may not have to make a bet on the final roll. As an example, in the first round of a tournament I faced all crapshooters and no tournament experts. Two people from my table were going to advance to the second round. There were ten of us at the table, and we all started with $500. Going into the final roll I was BR1 with $765. BR2 had about $720, and BR3 had about $680. Three other players had more than $500. I was prepared to bet my whole bankroll in the manner that would give me the best chance to advance to the next round, but instead I just kept my chips in the rack. The reason is none of my opponents made a bet that could hurt me. No matter what the dice showed, I would be BR1 after the final bets were decided. My opponents offered me a lock, so I smiled and accepted it.

Generally, however, your opponents are more contentious. They tend to make large bets on the final roll of the dice. You may be BR1 going into the final roll, but if enough of your opponents bet enough different ways on the final roll, some of them will lose and some will win and those that win may pass you. So accept that you are going to have to bet all your chips on the final roll. Your goal is to bet your chips in such a manner that you have as high a chance of advancing as possible.

There are 36 possible rolls of two dice. (See table 8, page 203.) Make bets such that as many as possible of those 36 will allow you to advance to the next round.

Bets With a Big Lead

If you have a lead of more than the max on a field bet, you have at least a 24/36 chance of advancing to the next round, and possibly you have a lock. The worst case is if you have to bet first on the final roll, and your opponents will be able to bet after your bets are locked in; in that situation, you should be a 24/36 favorite to advance.

The way you get 24/36 is by buying or placing all the numbers for large enough amounts so that your opponents cannot bet enough to beat you if a 4, 5, 6, 8, 9, or 10 rolls.

For example, suppose the maximum place bet is $300, you have $1501, and your nearest competitor has $1200. If you place the 6 and 8 for $60 each, the 5 for $100, the 9 for $300, and you buy the 4 and 10 for $300 each, you advance to the next round if any of those numbers rolls, which happens 24 out of 36 times.

The total required to make the above bets is $1150. If your bankroll is less than $1150, you need a lead of more than $350 to get the same 24/36 probability of advancing. Suppose you have $1101 and your nearest competitor has $750. You do not have to place 6 or 8; if one of them rolls, you advance. You place the 5 for $50; now if 5 rolls you advance. You place the 9 for $250, and you buy the 4 and 10 for $300 each and now you have your 24 ways to win out of 36 rolls.

When you have a lead and you are placing numbers to get your 24/36 probability of winning, do not make any bets that lose to a 4, 5, 6, 8, 9, or 10. For example, do not bet the field.

For a $300 maximum, the numbers of the above paragraphs apply. You have to figure out the amounts to bet at a tournament with other than a $300 maximum. For example, suppose the maximum place bet on 6 or 8 is $600. An opponent who places the 6 for $600 will win $700 if a 6 rolls. What do you need to win on a 6 to stay ahead of somebody who wins $700? If your lead is $500, you need to win at least $200, which suggests placing the 6 and 8 for $180 each to win $210.

The reason for getting a max field bet ahead to grab off all the numbers is if you have a lead of less than a field bet, someone who bets the max in the field and buys or places the 4, 9, and 10 for the max will beat you unless you bet the field also. But you cannot bet the field if you want to win on a 5, 6, or 8. The only way you can win on all six of those numbers is to be so far ahead that you can win even if someone else wins a max field bet.

Bluff

If your lead is less than a max field bet, you do not have enough of a lead to grab off the 4, 5, 6, 8, 9, and 10 for yourself if your opponents make optimal bets. However, your opponents are human and they have to make their bets in limited time. If you have an obvious lead, and you make place bets on all the numbers, your opponents generally assume that you will win if any of those numbers roll. They will not try to take any of them away from you by making bigger bets on them. Even if this bluff will not work every time, it works often enough to justify its use. Possible combinations of bets are covered later in this chapter as "details of last-roll strategies."

Bets if You Have a Small Lead

If for some reason you are unable to get the lead you want, pick out one group of dice rolls to cover. Put yourself in the position that if one of your numbers is rolled, you win the table; and accept the fact that if another number is rolled, you lose. Which numbers you bet and how you bet them depend on how much money you have, how much money your competitors have, how many other people have more money than you, your betting position, and the degree of expertise you think your opponents have.

Bets if You Are Not BR*

If you are still in contention on the last roll but have not managed to be BR*, you should still make large bets and give your opponent a chance to screw up. More than once I have seen situations where BR1 had a big lead and could have had a lock by simply matched BR2's bets, but instead gave BR2 a chance to win.

Hop Bets

There is one crap bet that has seldom been used in tournament craps, just as doubling down on anything formerly was seldom used in tournament blackjack. The strategy is hop bets. Hop bets give the casino a hefty 17%, but sometimes they give you the best probability of winning the table.

Hop bets give you more bang for the buck than place bets. This means if you want to make both hop bets and place bets but you do not have enough money to go to the max on both, you have a better chance to catch someone (or stay ahead of someone) if your number rolls by making max hop bets and putting the remainder of your money on place bets.

Ten Seconds

You must make your bets fairly quickly. The stick man is not going to pause for you to look around the table to decide what to bet. If the final roll is announced, you are BR* and the other players are not making bets that might displace you, smile and wait for the stick man to say "No more bets." But if you know you are going to have to make bets on the final roll, as soon as the final roll is announced you should immediately place all your chips on the felt to make sure you get your bets made. Otherwise "No more bets" will be called and you will lose.

Betting Position

Betting position is very important. If you are not required to bet in any particular order, then if you are BR* you have the luxury of making the final bet; that is, you can wait to see if any of your opponents makes a bet to challenge you, and if there is such a bet then you make your own bets.

In some tournaments you must bet in order on the final roll, starting with either the shooter or the person to the shooter's left. Late bettors definitely have a big edge over early bettors. A bad situation to be in is to have someone you want to beat who is ahead of you in chips, betting after you on the final roll, and matching your bets. You have much the worse of it, but at least you have a small chance if you do not make the mistake of allowing that person to match your bets and at the same time make optimal bets. You must make bets that give that person a choice of making optimal bets and giving you a chance to win, or matching your bets and accepting less of a chance of winning the tournament than what s/he otherwise could have had. For example, with one winner per table, you are BR2, and BR1 bets after you, you should not place all the numbers. If you do, BR1 will smile and match your bets.

Details of Last-Roll Strategies

Start deciding what your final bets will be with about five minutes or five rolls to go. By the time the final roll arrives, you should have already decided exactly what numbers you are going to bet. If your lead is large enough you are ready to bet all the numbers. If you are ahead but your lead is small, or if you are not BR*, you are ready to make another set of bets. Try to grab off as many of the 36 possible rolls as you can. Do it by making bets that go well together. Here are the details on some last-roll strategies you might consider using.

All the Numbers

If you need to make a bet because if you sit on your chips you lose, but you have an obvious lead, then place the 5, 6, 8, and 9 and buy the 4 and 10. If you have a big enough lead you may not need to go to the max on each number as explained earlier in this chapter, but if you do not have time to do the arithmetic just spread your whole bankroll over all the numbers. If the last roll is a 7 you are dead whether or not you fine-tune the size of your final bets.

Five-Six-Eight

If you are BR* with a small lead and you find that you must make a bet, you can tie up the 5, 6, and 8 for a 14/36 probability of winning the table. If you are not BR* but enough of the people you are trying to catch are not betting those numbers, take the 5, 6, and 8.

Place the 5, 6, and 8 for the max. If you do not have that many chips, split what you do have into three equal place bets. (Best is 5/17 of your bankroll on 5, and 6/17 on each of 6 and 8.)

If you still have money left, bet the big 6 and big 8. These bets are similar to hop bets in that your opponents might not think of betting them.

If you have to, bet the hard 6 on the hop and hard 8 on the hop for small amounts each, and make small hop bets on all the other ways to make 5, 6, and 8. That means max hop bets on each of 1-4, 2-3, 1-5, 2-4, 2-6, and 3-5. If you have to make hop bets and have to choose between hop bets and place bets, remember that hop bets give more bang for the buck.

Another possibility is to lock up the 6 and 8 only, for a 10/36 chance of winning the table. Or you can lock up the 5 and 6, or 5 and 8, for a 9/36 chance of winning the table.

Four-Nine-Ten

You can tie up the 4, 9, and 10 for a probability of winning the table of 10/36. Start with a max bet in the field. With what money you have left, place the 9 and buy the 4 and 10. A proper split is about 7/24 of your remaining money on each of 4 and 10, and about 10/24 of it on 9.

If you have to, bet the hard 4 hopping and the hard 10 hopping, and 1-3, 3-6, 4-5, and 4-6 hopping.

Seven

If you are a long way behind BR*, bet on 7. The probability of a 7 rolling is 6/36. There is almost no limit to how much of a gap you can make up by betting on 7 if your opponents have the table covered with bets that lose to 7.

Start with max hop bets on 1-6, 2-5, and 3-4, and a max bet on any seven.

If there is a point, bet the max on the come. If the shooter is coming out for a point, bet the max on pass.

If you still have money left to bet on 7, buy behind the 6 and 8, putting up 5% commission on the payoffs. I.e. lay $120 to win $100, and give the casino $5 commission. Bet as much money behind the 6 and 8 as you can; you get more bang for the buck behind those numbers than behind 4, 5, 9, or 10.

If you still have money left to bet on 7, buy behind the 5 and 9. Put up $150 to win $100 and give the casino a 5% commission on the payoff, which means putting up $155 to win $100. Bet as much behind the 5 and 9 as you can.

If you still have money left after making max bets behind the 5, 6, 8, and 9, buy behind the 4 and 10. Put up $200 to win $100 and give the casino a 5% commission, which means risking $205 to win $95.

Craps

If so many people ahead of you are already betting on 7 that you would not rise to BR* even if a 7 rolled, bet on craps. Bet the max in the field, the max on each crap roll and on any crap, and the max on don't come. Your probability of getting a crap roll is 4/36.

Hopping Hardways

"Hopping hardways" is a combination bet guaranteed to confuse your opponents. With a $300 max, you need $810 to make these bets, and if you win the net amount of your win is $700 to $735. Your probability of winning is 10/36.

Here are the hopping-hardways bets. Buy the 4 and 10 for $300 each. Bet the hard 4 and hard 10 hopping for $10 each, and bet each of the easy ways to make 4 and 10 (1-3 and 4-6) for $20 hopping. And bet all other hardways, 1-1, 3-3, 4-4, and 6-6, for $30 each hopping. The beauty of this combination of bets is your net win is at least $700 no matter which of your ten rolls occurs. I do not know of another way to cover ten rolls with such a high win for such a small investment.

You might also make a modification of the hopping-hardways strategy. For example, if the person you are trying to catch has such a large bet on 6 that you cannot catch up by hitting hard 6 hopping, then make all the hopping hardways bets except do not bet on hard 6. This means you will bet $780 total instead of $810, you will have 9/36 probability of winning; and if you win, the amount you win will be at least $730.

Likewise if you need to catch up more than $700 but less than $730, omit the bet on hopping hard 6. If you need to catch up more than $730 but less than $760, omit the hopping hard 8 and hopping hard 6, and still have 8/36 chance of winning the table.

The best time to use the hopping hardways is when someone at the other end of the table is trying to lock you out by matching your bets. If you simply throw $200 on the come, that person will easily be able to match your bet. But a complicated combination of eleven bets that person probably will not be able to match.

CHAPTER 15
MORE ON CRAP
TOURNAMENTS

If you see me as an opponent, you can be sure you are taking on me alone; I will not be participating in any multi-person effort to beat you.

Playing Against Teams

Suppose you look around the table and see people who you think may be playing together. Is there any strategy they can use to get an extra advantage over you? The answer is yes: As soon as one of them gets ahead of you by even as little as a dollar, s/he can match your bets to stay ahead of you. If that person does manage to match every bet you make, the best you can hope for is second place; you have no chance to be BR1. That is not a comfortable situation to be in.

If half the players on the final table play together as a team, they can almost certainly capture first prize—they will not win it every time but they will win it considerably more often than if they played independently — if their opponents do not know how to defend against them.

If you make small bets until a competing team member gets ahead of you and starts matching your bets, you are reduced to making bets that hopefully that person will not be able to match. You will be making or changing bets at the last instant, and you will be making bets you otherwise would prefer not to make. You and your opponent will be switching bets back and forth constantly and holding up the game, which does not make dealers and supervisors happy.

A much better defense, if you think you are up against a team, is to take the offensive. Go all-in early, get ahead of all members of the team, and stay ahead. Correlate with whichever team member is the most serious threat.

A team does not have an edge over you if you play in this manner. Sure you will bust out frequently, but you will win your share of tournaments the same as if the team members played individually. But if you do not play aggressively, the team will win more than its share and you will win less than your share.

Casino Comportment

You have a big edge in crap tournaments when you play against people who are not tournament experts. It would be nice to see those people come back for future crap tournaments. So do what you can to help them enjoy themselves in this tournament. Before the session, smile and say "Hello." After the session, listen sympathetically to their hard-luck stories and refrain from criticizing their play. During the session, make your bets quickly. Root for the shooter even if you are betting on the don't side. When you lose, smile and congratulate the victors. When you win, smile and act as if it is all luck.

When you are correlating to stay ahead of someone, do it subtly. Act as if you are making a bet because you think the bet will win. Make your opponent feel complimented that you are taking advice on where to bet. As you bet $100 in the field to approximately match your most serious opponent's $150 field bet, you might say something like: "You are right; a field roll is due." Unless your lead is tiny, do not match an opponent precisely bet for bet, because that might make the person unhappy.

The result should be that your opponents like you. If you advance and they do not, and they root for you to win again on the next round, you have done a good job on comportment.

Bets Off Instead of Down

Here is a sneaky ploy you cannot use very often because it is at odds with what you should be trying to do in comportment. Suppose you had some place bets working and now you do not want action on them anymore. You do not have to take the place bets down and put the chips in the rack; you can simply tell the dealer you want your bets off until you say they are back on. When you do this, the dealer marks your bets with a little button saying "off." Now when the dice roll your bets do not win and do not lose. If your opponents are not alert, they might not notice that your place bets are not in danger of being lost, and they might not realize you will beat them if the next roll is a 7. Some crapshooters do not know that bets can be on the layout but not at risk.

Likewise, watch your opponent's place bets and if any of them are off, treat those bets as if the opponent had those chips in the rack.

Crap tournament strategy is complicated because it depends on so many things: the house rules, the skill of your opponents, position of you and your most serious competitors at the table, how many chips each competitor has, and so forth. You may face situations that are slightly different from any discussed in this book. One of the things to keep in mind in such a situation is that generally you do not have a lock. You are simply trying to grab as many of the 36 possible rolls of the dice as you can. You have generally got to give your opponents a chance to beat you; accept that. Do not think in terms of making the perfect play; think in terms of making a play that gives you a good chance to win.

Another thing to keep in mind is that if you are up against tournament experts and deciding whether to make a bet, you generally are better off betting your money than keeping it in the rack. Against people who are not tournament experts, you generally are better off assuming they will keep their established betting patterns.

CHAPTER 16
MORE ON CRAPS

Craps is the most important dice game offered in casinos. There is no way you can get an edge at the

Table 8
All Possible Rolls of Two Dice

1 two	(1-1)	
2 threes	(1-2, 2-1)	
3 fours	(1-3, 2-2, 3-1)	
4 fives	(1-4, 2-3, 3-2, 4-1)	
5 sixes	(1-5, 2-4, 3-3, 4-2, 5-1)	
6 sevens	(1-6, 2-5, 3-4, 4-3, 5-2, 6-1)	
5 eights	(2-6, 3-5, 4-4, 5-3, 6-2)	
4 nines	(3-6, 4-5, 5-4, 6,3)	
3 tens	(4-6, 5-5, 6-4)	
2 elevens	(5-6, 6-5)	
1 twelve	(6-6)	

standard game short of cheating; and I certainly advise against bringing your own dice to switch into the game.

The only times you can make money playing craps are tournaments and special promotions.

Crap promotions are easy to analyze because there are only 36 possible rolls of the dice, as shown in table 8. You can list all possible outcomes to figure your edge precisely. This chapter has some examples.

Rainbow Promotion: 3:2 On Naturals

On the evening of 29 March 1982, I got a phone call from Alison Green. She had just seen a newspaper ad for the Rainbow in Henderson — the club was going to pay 3:2 on naturals at craps the next day.

Player's Edge

A natural at craps is 7 or 11 on the comeout roll. Six 7s plus two 11s out of 36 possible rolls is 8/36. The bonus payoff is 50% so divide by two, leaving 4/36 or 11.1%. Subtracting the initial house edge of 1.4% leaves the player an advantage of 9.7% per come-out roll. The average number of rolls per decision at craps is 3.376, making the player's edge about 2.9% per roll of the dice. The maximum bet was $50, so the average roll of the dice would be worth about $1.44 to a player betting the max. The pace of a crap game is usually 90 rolls an hour or more, making a player's time worth $130 an hour or more at the Rainbow promotion. So I flew to Las Vegas.

The Party

The Rainbow had only one crap table, and it was open only one shift — 3 PM to 11 PM. At the start of the party the table was half full, with only a few $50 bettors.

The pace was about 120 rolls per hour, making my time worth over $170 per hour.

By 7 PM the table was full. Most of the players were people who normally prefer blackjack or poker. Few players were making come bets or buying numbers, so the pace quickened to as much as 270 rolls per hour — increasing the value of my time to almost $390 per hour. I could not afford to visit the restroom.

The Party Ended

The party was great fun while it lasted. The number of $50 line bets topped out at sixteen. Shortly after 8 PM one player shot eleven straight passes, and that pretty much doomed the giveaway. The club ran out of $25 chips — the players around the crap table had them all. Some of the players took green chips to the cashier thinking to recycle them, but the cashier ran out of $100 bills. The crap game continued, but the pace was leisurely because the $50 and $75 payoffs were being made with $5 chips. Then the club ran out of $5 chips too — each blackjack table had 20 or 30, and the rest belonged to the crapshooters.

At about 9 PM, after having lost over $30,000 at craps, the owner changed the rules. Henceforth the bonus payoff would be limited to bets of $5 or less. The $50 bettors picked up their winnings and headed for the cashier. (And the restroom.)

By now the cashier had come up with enough $100s and $20s to pay off most of the crapshooters, but the final four people in line — with $10,000 in chips among them — had their choice of accepting payment in small bills and coins, accepting a check, or taking a receipt and coming back the next day after the casino owner withdrew cash from a bank account.

Push On 6-6 On a Come-Out Roll

Chuck Wenner is a casino executive who thinks up coupon promotions that become legendary. He was responsible for the $950 coupon book at the Marina in 1989 and the $615 coupon book at Westward Ho in 1985. Two of the coupons at each casino were for craps.

One coupon was good for a push on 6-6 on a come-out roll. Normally, a pass-line bet loses to 6-6 on a come-out roll. The coupon was kept until 6-6 rolled, and when the dealer reached for your bet you saved it by proffering the coupon.

On average it takes 36 bets to use the coupon. If you make a bet on either the pass line or the come so that you can bet on every roll of the dice, it takes an average of 36 rolls to use the coupon. One bet saved per 36 rolls is 2.778%. The casino's normal edge over you on those bets is 1.414%. (The precise casino edge is 28/1980 on pass and come bets, and 27/1980 on don't pass and don't come bets.) Subtraction shows that with this coupon you could play craps with an edge of 1.364%, and on average you could place 36 bets before using the coupon (and thus losing your edge). Multiplication shows that this coupon had a net expected value of 49% of a bet. Westward Ho allowed bets of up to $100 and Marina allowed bets of up to $500, so this was a nice coupon indeed.

One problem with this coupon is the time it takes to use it. At 90 rolls an hour, it takes about 24 minutes for 36 rolls. If you are betting big enough, you do not mind investing 24 minutes to get an edge of almost half a bet. When Marina lowered the maximum bet saved by the coupon to $5, playing craps with the coupon meant having an edge of $2.45 for 24 minutes of play. And of course there is risk involved. Sometimes the 6-6 comes right away, but it can take a long time.

I used the Marina's $5-max coupon once. I bet $5 on the pass line or the come to have a chance on every roll to use the coupon. The dice kept rolling and rolling, but no 6-6. I was winning, and to appear to be a gambler I started taking odds (zero percentage for the casino—just more variance). By the time 6-6 rolled and I finally got to use my coupon, an hour and a half had passed and I had won $460. That represents $2.45 of expected win and $457.55 of random deviation.

Push on 5 In the Field

The other Chuck Wenner coupon for craps allowed you to save a field bet when a 5 rolled. This coupon was similar to the push-on-6-6 coupon in several respects. You kept it until you needed it. It exactly reversed the odds, giving you an edge equal to that normally enjoyed by the casino over customers who make field bets. It was worth half a bet. You could bet up to $100 at Westward Ho and $500 at Marina.

This is a much more desirable coupon than the push-on-6-6 coupon. The reason is the expected value per roll is much higher. It takes an average of nine rolls of the dice to get a 5, and you play with an edge of 5.6% until a 5 appears.

Double Trouble At Nob Hill

Starting in 1985, Nob Hill in Las Vegas had a promotion it called "double trouble." When a certain red light went on, slot machine jackpots paid double, naturals at blackjack paid double, and field bets at craps won extra if certain numbers were rolled.

Double pay on naturals at blackjack is nice; it gives you an extra 2.3%. But if you stumble upon a promotion like this, do not simply rush in and play blackjack. Check out the other games too. At Nob Hill's double trouble, the best game to play was craps.

Normally on field bets in Las Vegas Strip casinos, the 2 and 12 win double, 3, 4, 9, 10, and 11 win even money, and 5, 6, 7, and 8 lose. The 36 possible rolls of the dice include 20 losers and 16 winners, and the winners pay 18 units. Thus the casino's edge is 2/36, or 5.6%.

Originally at Nob Hill's double trouble, field bets won double on rolls of 4 or 10, and triple on rolls of 2 or 12. There still were 20 losing rolls and 16 winning rolls, but the 16 winners paid 26 units. Thus you had an edge of 6/36 or 16.7% for three minutes out of every hour. Tokes encouraged dealers to be speedy; five or six rolls per three minutes was the norm.

Then Nob Hill changed the rules to "craps in the field pay double." This meant double pay for 2, 3, and 12, which is extra pay only for the 3. There still were 20 losers and 16 winners, but the 16 winners paid 20 units. This was zero edge to either side, so I stopped playing craps at Nob Hill.

Crapless Craps

Would you like to play in a crap game where you cannot lose on the come-out roll? You can find such a game at Vegas World: "crapless craps."

In crapless craps, if you roll 2, 3, or 12 on your first roll, that number becomes your point just as if you had rolled 4, 5, 6, 8, 9, or 10. On subsequent rolls if you roll your point before you roll a 7, you win; if you roll a 7 before your point, you lose. The possibility of winning on a come-out crap roll is worth 4.4% to you.

There is one other difference between crapless craps and regular craps. In crapless craps, 11 on the come-out roll is not an automatic winner. Instead it is a point, and to win you must roll 11 again before rolling 7; if you roll 7 before 11, you lose. Having 11 as a point costs you 8.3%.

The net result is that crapless craps gives the house a bigger advantage than regular craps. Passline bets at regular craps give the house an edge of about 1.4%; at crapless craps the house edge is about 5.4%.

Crap Challenge

I sometimes receive letters advertising systems for craps. Part of one letter says, "I challenge any casino, newspaper, magazine, or any other group to beat me over a 30 day period anywhere. If they beat my method, I want $10,000 and an apology."

This challenge appealed to me. So I wrote to the author to tell him I accepted his challenge. I offered to let him pick any casino in Las Vegas. I offered to deposit $10,000 in cash with the casino, and told him that I would expect him to match it with $10,000 of his own money. If he is ahead after 30 days of play, the $20,000 is his; otherwise, it is mine. I insisted on at least two hours of play per day, and would have allowed him to play more than two hours if he wanted. I also insisted that he play only with markers so that I could monitor his performance.

The casino test never took place because the system seller never responded to my acceptance of his challenge.

Apparently the challenge was bogus. Can his crap system be other than bogus? The sad truth is there is no such thing as a crap system that gives you an edge over the casino.

Making a Living At Craps

A reader writes, "I would like to make a living by 'gambling' in the casinos, especially playing craps. What is the best way to do it? I would like to travel, especially in Latin America and the Far East, if I can support myself by gambling. I hope you can give me some guidance."

If you want to make a living at craps, get a job as a dealer. In spite of all the advertisements you receive assuring you that you can make big money at craps if you just buy a system, you are not going to be able to support yourself at craps. No crap system gives you an edge over the casino, and all crapshooters lose in the long run.

The only exception is if you learn to throw the dice in a manner that one of the cubes spins instead of tumbles. If you can control one die well enough that the number of your choosing comes up more than the usual 1/6 of the time, you might be able to make money as a customer at the crap table. I have never seen a demonstration of this skill, but I have heard about it from a number of reputable sources.

If you did learn to control a die, you would find yourself unwelcome in casinos. It takes a sharp casino employee to be able to distinguish a professional black-jack player from the gamblers, but the least sharp employee ought to be able to see that one die is spinning instead of tumbling.

SECTION C

BACCARAT

Baccarat

There are three different wagers

1. The Player: Pays even money
2. The Banker: Pays 95% of even money
3. The Tie: Pays 9 for 1

Two cards are dealt for both sides, the Player and the Bank. If the rules call for the Player to take a third card, s/he does. If the rules call for the Banker to take a third card, s/he does.

The value of each hand is the last digit of the sum. Face cards count zero. Example: 7+8 = 15; the value of this hand is 5. The hand with the larger value (i.e closer to 9) wins.

In case of a tie, only wagers placed on the tie win 9 for 1; there is no action on the wagers on the Player or the Bank.

Rules: Player

Player's First Two Cards	Player Action
0-1-2-3-4-5	Draw a card
6-7	Stand
8-9	Natural—both hands stand

Rules: Banker

When the Player stands on 6 or 7, the Banker draws on totals of 0-1-2-3-4-5 and stands on 6-7-8-9.

When the Player does not have a natural, the Banker draws on totals of 0-1-2. With 3 or more, the banker takes a third card in the following situations:

Banker's first two cards	Player's third card
3	anything but 8
4	2-3-4-5-6-7
5	4-5-6-7
6	6-7
7	stands no matter what player drew
8-9	natural—neither hand draws

CHAPTER 17
TOURNAMENT
BACCARAT

Baccarat tournament rules vary from tournament to tournament. Some are funny money with no commission taken from bank wins, and some are real money with the standard 5% commission taken from bank wins. Some have maximum bets equal to or greater than starting bankrolls, and some have maximum bets that are small compared to starting bankrolls. Number of

Table 9
Probabilities for Baccarat

Bank	.459
Player	.446
Tie	.095 (pays 8 to 1)

winners per table varies from one to six. Number of decks shuffled varies from one to five. Number of shoes played is one or two.

All tournaments have a cut card that defines the second-last hand. Some have a secret bet, and on some secret bets the only secret is the amount of the bet and not where the bet is placed.

Seat Selection

Seat selection in a baccarat tournament is important. The standard format is to play one shoe (or two), with bets placed in order starting with seat 1. After each hand, the next player bets first. The average hand uses 4.94 cards. In some tournaments the betting order does not change after a tie, in which case the betting order changes once per 5.46 cards. Since you know total cards used, you can find the expected number of times the betting order will change. If you know how many players per table, you can figure out which seat is most likely to bet first on the final hand if nobody busts out.

Edge Over Player to Left

The player to your left bets after you only once per number of players. With twelve players per table, you bet after the player to your left eleven times out of twelve. That means you have a big edge over that player. If you get ahead of the player to your left, you can match that person's bets eleven times out of twelve. If that person is ahead of you, you can bet the opposite way eleven times out of twelve. Therefore, do not worry if the person on your left gets ahead of you, as long as that person does not get too far ahead.

The opponent on your right, however, is a different matter. If that opponent wants to match your bets or bet opposite from you, s/he can do so eleven times out of twelve.

Best Bet

Whether a commission is taken or not, the best bet in baccarat tournaments is bank. Therefore, you generally want to bet bank. Tie is the worst bet. Bet it only on the last hand when you are trying to tie up the highest possible probability of winning the table.

Though you generally prefer to bet bank, there are at least two situations in which you should bet on player. One is if the opponent you are trying to catch already has a bet on bank; then you bet on player to get more swing for a given bet size. The other is if a commission is taken on winning bank bets and so few hands remain that paying a commission will leave you with odd chips you will not be able to bet; then if you bet on player you preserve your option of betting your whole bankroll.

Know How Many Hands Remain

Participants in baccarat tournaments generally are allowed to use pencil and paper. Use them to keep track of total cards remaining to be dealt. You can divide that number by five to estimate how many hands are yet to be played. You can figure out what your betting position will be on the final hand.

Watch the placement of the plastic card or cards that determine how many cards will be used. Sometimes the actual placement is different from what you were led to expect. For example, at one tournament the participants were told that plastic cards were to be placed at one and two decks, but they actually were inserted at about 40 and 80 cards. In another tournament, participants expected the stop card to be 15 cards from the end of the shoe but it was inserted a full deck from the end; that tournament ended way too soon for anyone who was not watching the placement of the stop card.

Secret Bets

If you get one and only one secret bet, save it in case you need it on the final hand. You may not need it; in baccarat, unlike blackjack, when you bet last you have absolutely no reason to make a secret bet.

If you get more than one secret bet, save one for the final hand. The others you might use when you have to bet first or second on the final time the betting order comes around to you before the final hand, or you might save them for the hands immediately before the final one. Do not use a secret bet earlier than the final time the betting order comes around to you.

Just because you want to make a big bet is no reason to do it secretly. For example, in one baccarat tournament I had 900, five other players had 1100 to 1400, three players were going to advance to the next round, and we had plenty of hands left to play. I decided to bet 300, and if that bet lost I intended to bet my final 600. So what if everyone knew what I was betting? I did not use a secret bet.

Betting Strategy: To Last Ten Hands

If the Maximum Bet is Low

If the max is low compared to your bankroll, get the BR* position early; if you are knocked out of the BR* spot, immediately try to regain it.

If the Maximum is High

If the max bet is high in relation to your bankroll, you have the luxury of waiting until the last five or ten hands to become BR*. If you are BR*, stick with optimal proportional betting. An exception is in a two-person game when you can match your opponent's bet. Another exception is a no-commission game with only one winner; you can be fairly confident that your initial bankroll will not hold up as BR1, so you might make slightly larger bets.

If you are not BR*, bet for a swing if you know your present bankroll will be inadequate or if a good opportunity presents itself. An example of when you know your present bankroll will be inadequate is when there will be but one winner per table. In that case it is best to bet aggressively at the start.

A good opportunity is what Blair Rodman had with about two dozen hands to go in the final round of a Las Vegas Hilton no-limit tournament. Rodman had been making minimum bets; his 25,000 bankroll was virtually unchanged from what he started with. Several players were ahead of him. The two leaders, with 75,000 and 70,000, were betting wildly. Then BR2 bet 20,000 on bank, and BR1 followed with a bet of 25,000 also on bank. Rodman could have bet small, and he would have had a 44.6% chance of having half as much as the leaders, and a 45.9% chance of having one fourth as much as the leaders. Instead, he went all in on player. That gave him a 44.6% chance of being virtually tied for the lead with two other players and a 45.9% chance of busting out. His probability of winning the tournament was considerably higher by going all-in when he did.

Betting Strategy: Ten Hands To Last Hand

You want to be BR* or better going into the last hand.

If there are many contestants and few advancing to the next round, your opponents probably will be betting aggressively and you can feel confident that your initial bankroll will not hold up as BR*. Bet aggressively yourself, starting about five hands from the end.

If there is no secret bet, figure out your last-hand betting position. If you will be betting early on the last hand, you must be more solid going into that last hand than if you will be betting late.

If You Are BR* or Better

If you bet first, bet small on bank (meaning 1.4% or less of your bankroll if no commission, and the minimum if the casino takes a commission). If you bet after the people vying for the BR* spot, bet with the flow in a conservative manner.

If You Are Not BR*

If you do not have the bankroll position you want, and if you do not have to bet ahead of all the people you are trying to catch, make a bet that will give you a chance to catch up. It is best to bet bank, but if the people you are trying to catch have already bet bank, then bet on player.

It is best to bet a fraction of your bankroll that allows a betting progression: 1/7, 1/3, or all (see chapter 4). If the max is so low that you cannot bet that fraction, then bet the max.

Example

At a final table in Aruba we each started with 100,000 and the max was only 10,000. We were playing one eight-deck shoe, which meant about 80 hands. I was trying to be BR1.

On the first hand, over half the players bet the max. I did too and I lost, so I continued to bet 10,000 per hand. I bet on bank unless everyone betting ahead of me was already on bank, in which case I bet on player.

After ten hands my 100,000 had shrunk to 70,000, the smallest bankroll on the table. Then I started to win. When I bet on bank, bank won. When I bet on player, player won. After winning eleven max bets in a row to bring my bankroll up to 180,000, I finally got the BR1 spot.

As soon as I became BR1, I cut back to 100 to 2000 and bet only on bank. BR2, my only close competitor, sat immediately to my left. He continued to bet 5000 to 8000 per hand. If he bet big on bank, I bet 2000 on bank. If he bet big on player, I bet 100 on bank. If I bet ahead of him, I bet 1000 on bank. We both fluctuated downward, but he rejoined the pack while I dropped only to 160,000 and stayed BR1.

Last-Hand Betting Strategies

Which strategy you should use depends on the number of players left in contention, how many winners per table, the rank of your bankroll, and whether you get to make a secret bet. Betting position also matters unless your last bet is completely secret.

Every last-hand strategy includes a max bet on tie, but if losing a max bet on tie could drop you behind someone you don not want to fall behind, then bet what you can afford on tie instead of the max. Bet on tie on the last hand only. Do not bet on tie prior to the last hand.

Though the following strategies say "max," if you are BR* you do not actually have to make a full max bet on whichever of player or bank you select. It is sufficient to bet the max minus your lead plus your tie bet plus a chip. In other words, your minimum bet should be an amount sufficient to beat an opponent that makes a max bet the same way you do, assuming that opponent does not bet on tie.

Random Max

Make a max bet on either bank or player and make a max bet on tie. One way to select which to bet is to glance at the second hand on your wristwatch; if the second hand points to twelve or six or to the right, bet bank. If the second hand points to the left, bet player. Thus your choice is strictly random and does not depend whatsoever on any prediction of which way your chief opponent is betting. Note that you should be slightly more likely to bet on bank than on player. If you cannot make a secret bet, do not use the random-max strategy.

Max on Bank and Tie

Bet the max on bank and the max on tie.

Max on Player and Tie

Bet the max on player and the max on tie.

Max on Tie

Make a max bet on tie. If you are also required to bet on bank or player, bet the minimum on bank.

Last Hand, One Winner, You Are BR1, No Secret Bet

If someone who can catch you will bet after you, bet max on bank and tie.

If only BR2 has a shot at you but must bet before you, lock up a win.

Last Hand, N Winners, No Secret Bet

If you have a lock, smile. A lock might mean matching the bet of someone to your left.

If you bet early and do not have a lock going into the last hand, but you are BR*, bet max on bank and tie.

If in spite of your best intentions you are not BR* going into the last hand, make a bet that gives you a chance. If you are not BR* and you have to bet first, bet max on player and tie.

Last Hand, One Winner, Secret Bet

If anybody bets after you, make a secret bet.

You Are BR1 in a Two-Person Game

"Two-person," means only BR2 has a chance to catch you; BR3 is more behind than can be won in one hand.

If BR3 is more behind than can be caught up in one hand even if you lose a max bet, use the random-max strategy.

If BR3 is less than two max bets behind you, then modify the random-max strategy to make the amount of your random bet equal to the most you can bet without giving BR3 a shot at you.

For example, suppose you are in a tournament with a max of 16,000 on player or banker and 1000 on tie. You are BR1 with 32,000, BR2 has 28,000, BR3 has no more than 7400. Make a secret bet of 1000 on tie and at least 13,100 on whichever of player or bank you randomly select. If you cannot do the arithmetic because of too much pressure, just bet the max 1000 on tie and the max 16,000 on whichever of player or bank you randomly select.

Another example with the same limits: Suppose you are BR1 with 32,000, BR2 has 28,000, and BR3 has 10,000. Bet the max on tie and 10,900 on player or bank. (The least you can end up with is 20,100, so you have got BR3 locked out.)

You Are BR2 in a Two-Person Game

If you are a long way behind, or if BR3 is close enough so that BR1 has incentive to bet small to keep it a two-person game, use the random max strategy.

If you are close to BR1, BR3 is not a factor, and you can make a completely secret bet, bet max on tie. Your best chance to win is to hope BR1 makes a big bet on player or bank and loses. BR1 must make a bet before finding out what you are betting, and will assume you are making a substantial bet on either player or bank. BR1 will make a big bet to try to match you. Therefore, if you make a big bet on player or bank you have only got half as good a chance to win the table as you do betting tie only.

You Are BR1 in a Multi-Person Game

Bet max on bank and tie.

You Are BR2 Or Worse in a Multi-Person Game.
Find your exact position. If it is an even number, meaning you are BR2, BR4 or BR6, bet max on player and tie. If it is an odd number, meaning you are BR3, BR5, or BR7, bet max on bank and tie.

Last Hand, N Winners, Secret Bet

This strategy is based on the logic that of every two players making large bets, one will win and one will lose. Thus we have two contenders vying for each spot. Naturally you make a secret bet; except that if you are last to act, whether the other players see your bet does not matter.

You Are BRN in an N-Contender Game
If you have a lock, you sit on it and smile.

N+1 Contenders
If you have one of the top N-1 bankrolls, play as if you have a lock; bet max on tie. (You act as if you have a lock but you really do not; if everyone behind you bets the max on the same side and that side wins, you do not advance.) If you are BRN or worse, use the random max strategy.

For example, if six people are advancing and seven players are in contention going into the last hand, then BR5 and above do not have much to worry about. If you are BR6 or BR7, use the random max strategy.

N+2 Contenders
If you have one of the top N-1 bankrolls, play as if you have a lock, meaning bet max on tie. For example, if eight players are competing for six spots and you are BR5 or better, bet max on tie. If you are BR5 and you know for certain that BR6 and worse will bet big, then it makes no

difference whether you use the random max strategy or max on tie. The reason for betting max on tie is to give each of your opponents the opportunity to make a mistake.

If you are BRN, bet max on bank and tie. There is no reason to be random, because most likely one of your opponents will bet big one way and the other opponent will bet big the other way.

If you are just one spot worse than BRN, bet max on player and tie.

If you are two spots worse than BRN, you definitely should make a max bet on player or bank, and a bet on tie. If you think that one of your opponents possibly has bet the wrong side, bet the way that opponent should have bet. Otherwise you can bet max on bank and tie or you can make a random max bet.

N+3 Contenders

If you have one of the top N-2 bankrolls, bet max on tie. This is not a lock, but you should bet as though it were. For example, with seven contenders of which four will advance to the next round, you could be BR1 going into the final bet and not wind up as BR* if four or more of your opponents bet big the same way and that way wins. If you know for certain that all of your opponents will bet big on the final hand, you are better off betting big yourself because you have got a chance to be BR* even if you lose your final bet.

If you are BRN or the next higher bankroll, your spot is in jeopardy. Bet max on bank and tie.

If you are worse than that, bet max on player and tie.

More Contenders Yet

The same logic applies. The number of excess contenders minus one is the number of spots in jeopardy. If your spot is safe or right at the margin, bet max on tie. If your spot is in jeopardy, bet max on bank and tie. If you are worse than BRN, bet max on player and tie.

Miscellaneous Baccarat Items

Ten-Hand Playoff, No Secret Bet

Suppose you are in a playoff of say ten hands. The order of betting will change on bank wins and player wins, but not on ties. You would like to bet last on the tenth hand. Are you better off betting first or last on the first hand?

By 58% to 42%, you are better off betting first on the first hand. If there are zero or two ties in the first nine hands, you will bet last on the tenth hand. The probabilities of various numbers of ties in nine hands are shown in table 10, which is derived from table 9.

In a playoff consisting of an even number of hands, the person who bets first on the first hand has an edge. In a playoff consisting of an odd number of hands, the person who bets second on the first hand has an edge. A

Table 10
Number of Ties in Nine Hands

Tied Hands	Probability
0	.41
1	.38
2	.16
3	.04
4	.01

way to remember this is to choose your seat as if there will be zero ties in the playoff.

One Hand, Getting a Lead

Suppose you are tied with someone and you want to get a lead, any lead. Suppose that person bets first, with two chips on bank and one chip on tie. What do you bet? Your best bet is two chips on bank. You have a .905 chance of being a chip ahead of your opponent, and your opponent has .095 chance of being 8 chips ahead of you.

One-Hand Playoff, Secret Bet

Suppose you and another player are tied, and the two of you engage in a one-hand playoff with a secret bet. If you know what your opponent is betting, you can always make a bet that gives you more than 50% probability of winning the match. For example, suppose you know that your opponent is betting the max on bank and the max on tie; you bet the max on bank and win 90.5% of the time. Suppose you know your opponent is betting the max on bank; you bet max on player and tie and win 54.1% of the time. Suppose you know your opponent is betting the max on player and the max on tie; you bet the max on player and win 90.5% of the time. Suppose you know your opponent is betting the max on player; you bet max on bank and tie and win 55.4% of the time. We have come full circle: A beats B; B beats C; C beats D; and D beats A.

My recommendation in this situation: Randomly select between max on bank and max on player, hoping to catch your opponent with that same bet plus a tie bet.

SECTION D

KENO

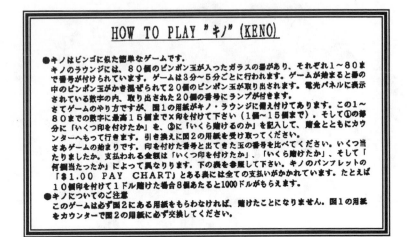

HOW TO PLAY "キノ" (KENO)

● キノはビンゴに似た簡単なゲームです.
　キノのラウンジには、80個のピンポン玉が入ったガラスの器があり、それぞれ1〜80まで番号が付けられています。ゲームは3分〜5分ごとに行われます。ゲームが始まると器の中のピンポン玉がかき混ぜられて20個のピンポン玉が取り出されます。電光パネルに表示されている数字の内、取り出された20個の番号にランプが付きます。
　さてゲームのやり方ですが、図1の用紙がキノ・ラウンジに備え付けてあります。この1〜80までの数字に最高15個までX印を付けて下さい（1個〜15個まで）。そして①の部分に「いくつ印を付けたか」を、②に「いくら賭けるのか」を記入して、賭金とともにカウンターへもって行きます。引き換えに図2の用紙を受け取ってください。
　さあゲームの始まりです。印を付けた番号と出てきた玉の番号を比べてください。いくつ当たりましたか。支払われる金額は「いくつ印を付けたか」、「いくら賭けたか」、そして「何個当たったか」によって異なります。下の表を参照して下さい。キノのパンフレットの「$1.00 PAY CHART」とある欄には全ての支払いがかかれています。たとえば10個印を付けて1ドル賭けた場合8個当たると1000ドルがもらえます。
● キノについてのご注意
　このゲームは必ず図2にある用紙をもらわなければ、賭けたことになりません。図1の用紙をカウンターで図2の用紙に必ず交換してください。

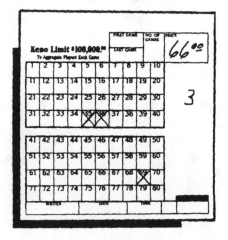

CHAPTER 18
TOURNAMENT
KENO

In keno you want to maximize your chance of winning the tournament. Set a goal and then select the ticket that gives you the maximum chance of hitting your goal. If you play more than one ticket per game, select separate numbers for each ticket. Select your numbers randomly so as to minimize ties with other competitors.

Setting a Goal

Here is a procedure for setting a goal. Start by finding the average ending bankroll. The casino keeps about 25% on keno wagers, giving about 75% back to the customers in the form of payoffs. So the average ending bankroll is the beginning bankroll minus 25% of a contestant's keno wagers. Multiply the average ending bankroll by the square root of the number of contestants.

This is a reasonable target to aim at to win the tournament. You might be able revise your goal as you get information about actual results achieved by tournament entrants.

Here is a numerical example. Suppose there are 100 contestants each wagering $1000. The average contestant will turn $1000 into $750. The square root of the number of contestants is 10. The product of $750 and 10 is $7500. The median winning score over many such keno tournaments probably will be about $7500, so you should aim to beat $7500.

Unfortunately, the winning score on a given keno tournament might be considerably less than or more than your target. There is a chance that you will hit your target and not win the tournament.

Maximum Chance of Hitting Your Goal

Your maximum chance of hitting your goal comes when you select tickets that will pay you either enough to make your goal or zero, but nothing in between. This means you should try to avoid tickets with a variety of payoffs. Best is winner-take-all tickets if they are available. Otherwise, you are better off selecting as few spots as possible.

Bet Late Games

Try to save your money for the final games. If you win early and your opponents find out about it, you set a target that might cause them to change their tickets to have a better chance to beat you. If one of your opponents wins big early, you can find out about it and revise your target.

Table 11
Probabilities of Hitting All

Spots	Payoff for hitting all	Probability of hitting all
1	3	.25
2	12	.0601
3	52	.0139
4	180	.00306
5	1000	.000645

Payoff Schedule

Table 11 is all the information about keno payoff schedules that you need to select your tickets.

The details of keno tournaments vary considerably from tournament to tournament. You may have to bet every game, or you might be able to sit out some games. It might be overall-winner format, or it might be a stated percentage of the entrants moving on to the next round. The following examples are illustrative of the variety of formats you will face.

Keno Example #1

The tournament is limited to 80 entrants, each of whom bets $500 in real money. Rebuys are allowed. The minimum ticket is $10.

Using the square root of the number of entrants times 75% of the $500 buy-in yields $3400 as an estimate of the winning total.

One possibility is a $20 four-spot, which pays off $3600 if all four spots hit. The probability of hitting at least one four-spot in 25 games is .0738. If someone chalks up a score higher than $3600, then immediately switch to a ticket that will win if it hits.

A better strategy is to save your whole $500 for the final game of the tournament. Then bet it all on tickets with three spots or less in a manner that either you finish with zero or you win the tournament. Betting $500 on a one-spot wins $1500. $500 on a two-spot wins $6000. $500 on a three-spot wins $26,000. If, for example, you have to beat a posted score of $7000, you can split your $500 into three three-spots.

If you save all your money for the final game, you might work out a schedule ahead of time that shows which tickets you will bet depending on the amount you need to win. A sample is shown in table 12, which assumes you have a total of $800 to bet. You can use table 12 yourself if a winning $1 one-spot pays $3, a winning $1 two-spot pays $12, a winning $1 three-spot pays $52, a winning $1 four-spot pays $180, and a winning $1 five-spot pays $1000. If you want to bet a different amount than $800, or if the keno game you are playing has different payoffs per $1, you will have to modify table 12.

Keno Example #2

The tournament has 125 entrants each of whom wagers $1000 of credits over 25 games. Contestants must play one or two tickets every game until their $1000 is gone. Tickets can be changed only on games 11 and 21.

A reasonable target is $8400.

For each of the first 20 games, play a $10 five-spot. If all five spots hit, the payoff is $10,000. The probability of hitting five out of five at least once in 20 games is .0128.

Table 12
Tickets to Achieve Target

Payoff	Prob	Ticket(s)	Games
$1,200	.4375	$400 one-spot	two
2,400	.2500	$800 one-spot	one
4,160	.1306	two $80 three-spots	five
4,800	.1166	$400 two-spot	two
5,200	.1059	two $100 three-spots	four
6,448	.0817	$124 three-spot & $36 four-spot	five
6,916	.0806	two $133 three-spots	three
7,800	.0732	$650 two-spot & $150 three-spot	one
7,904	.0706	$152 three-spot & $8 five-spot	five
8,320	.0676	$160 three-spot	five
9,000	.0630	$750 two-spot & $50 four-spot	one
9,600	.0601	$800 two-spot	one
9,880	.0569	$190 three-spot & $10 five-spot	four
10,400	.0545	$200 three-spot	four
10,712	.0498	$206 three-spot & $60 four-spot	three
13,000	.0430	$253 three-spot & $13 five-spot	three
13,832	.0411	$266 three-spot	three
16,120	.0335	$310 three-spot & $90 four-spot	two
19,760	.0289	$380 three-spot & $20 five-spot	two
20,800	.0276	$400 three-spot	two
32,240	.0169	$620 three-spot & $180 four-spot	one
39,520	.0145	$760 three-spot & $40 five-spot	one
41,600	.0139	$800 three-spot	one
47,880	.0092	$266 four-spot	three
61,000	.0074	$339 four-spot & $61 five-spot	two
80,000	.0064	two $80 five-spots	five

If someone hits a ticket for more than $10,000 during the first 10 games, for games 11-20 bet a ticket of five spots or less and costing $20 or less that will make you the leader if it hits.

If your five-spot hits during the first 10 games and you are the leader, switch to $10 four-spots for games 11-20 because when your opponents find out about your big hit, they probably will try to beat you by a large amount. Against good tournament players you might switch to $10 one-spots because good players might try to beat you by just a small margin.

Games 21-25: You have Hit a Five-Spot And You Lead

Just in case your opponents are trying to beat your posted score by $1000 or $2000, you might bet a single one-spot for your remaining $800.

Games 21-25: You Trail

You have $800 left to bet. How you bet it depends on what you think you need to win to be numero uno. Redefine your target as the high score so far or something in the $6000 to $8000 range, depending on how many dollars you think your opponents have yet to bet. Select your bet from table 12. For example, if you need a payoff of $10,000, go with a $200 three-spot and your money lasts four games.

If you bet two tickets per game, pick totally separate numbers.

Inferior tickets have been omitted from table 12. For example, two $100 four-spots for four games has .0242 probability of a payoff of $18,000. A $400 three-spot for two games has a higher probability of a higher payoff, so you should never select two $100 four-spots.

Keno Example #3

The entry fee is $100, and all entry fees are returned as prize money. Buy-ins are $100 each, and each entrant with money left must bet each game.

First Round

The first round consists of two sessions of four hours of play each, which means at least 30 games per session. Entrants buy in for $100 each session. Minimum ticket price is $5. Advancement to the second round is based on entrant's bankroll, which is buy in plus winnings minus losses for that session. Advancing to the second round are: ten entrants from the first session, twenty from the second session, and ten more with the highest cumulative bankroll.

Second Round

Entrants buy in for $100. Minimum ticket price is $5. Twenty games are played, and ten entrants advance to the final round.

Final Round

Entrants buy in for $100. Minimum ticket price is $10. Ten games are played. Prize money is 70% to the winner, 20% to second, and 10% to third.

Strategy, First Round

To start, bet no more than two spots. You may bet five $1 one-spots. Or five $1 two-spots. Or a $5 one-spot. By turning your initial $100 into $75 each session, you have a good chance of advancing to the second round.

If it looks as if you will be a little short, on the final game split your bankroll into two equal parts and play a one-spot with each, finishing with 3/2 of what you started with if you hit either number. Or you can bet it all on one number, tripling your bankroll if that number hits.

If you need to increase your bankroll by a multiple other than 3/2 or 3, try to do it with two-spots on the last game. Do not overlap numbers on any of your two-spots. To find the number of two-spots to divide your money into, divide your bankroll by your goal and multiply by twelve. For example, if you have $75 and you think you need $300 to advance to the next round, $75/$300 is 1/4, and 1/4 times twelve is three. So divide your $75 into three two-spots of $25 each. If one of those two-spots hits, your payoff is $300.

Strategy, Second Round

Here your strategy depends on the number of good tournament players entered. If there are no other good tournament players, use the same strategy as you did on the first round — $5 per game on one-spots or two-spots, with going all in on the final bet if necessary.

I cannot imagine a keno tournament with no other good tournament players present. If there are only a handful of tournament experts in the second round, here is a progression you can use to give you a 68% chance of turning your $100 into $110 or so. Bet a $12 one-spot on the first game. If that loses, bet an $18 one-spot on the second game. If that loses, bet a $27 one-spot on the third game. If that loses, bet your last $43 as a one-spot on the fourth game. If you win any one of those bets, you have $124 or more, and you can immediately switch to five $1 one-spots to sit on your money.

"Sit on your money" means your bankroll drifts downward as the house edge nibbles away. Making $5 bets per game costs you an average of $1.25 per game.

I can imagine a keno tournament in which about half of the players in the second round are good tournament players. Here is a progression that gives you a 58% chance of turning your $100 into $130 or so. Bet a $21 one-spot on the first game. If that loses, bet a $32 one-spot. If that loses, bet your last $47 as a one-spot. If you win any one of those bets, you have $142 or $141, and you can immediately switch to five $1 one-spots to sit on your money.

If considerably more than half of the players in the second round are good tournament players, here is a progression that you can use to give you a 44% chance of turning your $100 into $160 or so, which should allow you to advance to the third round for certain: Bet a $40 one-spot on the first game. If that loses, bet your remaining $60 as a one-spot on the second game. If you win either bet you have $180, and you immediately switch to five $1 one-spots to sit on your money.

Strategy, Final Round

Go all-in on a one-spot on the first game. After that, as long as you have the lead, bet the minimum $10 per game on either one-spots or two-spots.

If someone pulls ahead of you by more than 80% of your bankroll, bet a $10 ticket that will give you the BR1 spot if all your numbers hit. If someone pulls ahead of you by less than 80% of your bankroll (example: you trail 400 to 280), immediately bet 40% of your bankroll as a one-spot; and if that bet loses, bet the remainder of your bankroll as a one-spot.

If you have the lead going into the final game, make a bet such that if it wins, you are likely to beat your most serious opponent even if that person also wins a bet. For example, if leading by $278 to $205, bet a $20 one-spot. The reason is your opponent probably will bet one-spots of $100 and $105; hitting the larger would yield $315, and you would beat that with $318 if your one-spot hits.

CHAPTER 19

KENO

PROBABILITIES

Calculation of keno probabilities is cumbersome, so for the January 1985 issue of *Winning Gamer* I worked them all out and put the results into an easy-to-use table, reproduced here as table 13.

Here is how to interpret the numbers in table 13. Each probability is expressed as two numbers separated by a hyphen. The probability is a decimal point and the first number separated by zeros equal to the second number. For example, the probability of hitting five numbers out of five is expressed in the table as 645-03. This means a decimal point and 645 separated by three zeros, or .000645. This method is used to simplify small probabilities. For example, the probability of hitting twelve numbers out of twelve is .00000000209, which is much easier to understand when expressed as 209-08.

Table 13
Keno Probabilities

Hits	Number of Spots Played					
	1	2	3	4	5	6
0	750-00	560-00	417-00	308-00	227-00	167-00
1	250-00	380-00	431-00	433-00	406-00	363-00
2		601-01	139-00	213-00	270-00	308-00
3			139-01	432-01	839-01	130-00
4				306-02	121-01	285-01
5					645-03	310-02
6						129-03

Hits	Number of Spots Played					
	7	8	9	10	11	12
0	122-00	883-01	637-01	458-01	327-01	232-01
1	315-00	266-00	221-00	180-00	144-00	114-00
2	327-00	328-00	316-00	295-00	268-00	238-00
3	175-00	215-00	246-00	267-00	278-00	280-00
4	522-01	815-01	114-00	147-00	179-00	206-00
5	864-02	183-01	326-01	514-01	741-01	994-01
6	732-03	237-02	572-02	115-01	202-01	322-01
7	244-04	160-03	592-03	161-02	361-02	703-02
8		435-05	326-04	135-03	411-03	102-02
9			724-06	612-05	284-04	954-04
10				112-06	106-05	543-05
11					160-07	167-06
12						209-08

Table 13 Continued

Hits	Number of Spots Played					
	13	14	15	16	17	18
0	164-01	115-01	802-02	555-02	382-02	260-02
1	888-01	685-01	523-01	395-01	295-01	218-01
2	207-00	176-00	148-00	122-00	996-01	800-01
3	273-00	259-00	240-00	218-00	195-00	171-00
4	227-00	242-00	250-00	251-00	247-00	237-00
5	126-00	152-00	176-00	197-00	214-00	226-00
6	475-01	676-01	863-01	108-00	131-00	153-00
7	123-01	199-01	299-01	425-01	576-01	748-01
8	218-02	418-02	733-02	120-01	183-01	267-01
9	260-03	608-03	127-02	241-02	423-02	699-02
10	201-04	597-04	152-03	343-03	703-03	133-02
11	943-06	381-05	123-04	340-04	829-04	183-03
12	240-07	148-06	650-06	228-05	678-05	178-04
13	246-09	308-08	207-07	984-07	372-06	119-05
14		257-10	350-09	254-08	131-07	532-07
15			234-11	345-10	270-09	149-08
16				180-12	286-11	241-10
17					112-13	193-12
18						535-15

You could use table 13 to evaluate all the ways to play keno in every casino, but you would be wasting your time. Back in 1964 when I turned 21 I naively thought that with so many different payoff schedules offered by so many casinos, there ought to be some mistakes, some keno games that actually gave the customer an edge. So I started analyzing keno schedules at different casinos, and I kept coming up with payback ratios of .79 to .81. Not only were there no mistakes in my favor, but there were only small deviations from a 20% casino edge. Today the situation is worse: The paybacks are less generous, and the casino edge is about 25% on almost every keno payoff schedule.

I still do the mathematics on special promotions. One that I heard about after it was over was a "1-cent sale" in which you paid the regular price for the first keno ticket and then bought another identical ticket for a penny. With a rule like that keno is fun, so keep your eyes open.

Continental Six-Spot

The only keno giveaway I have found out about soon enough to get in on myself was at the Continental in Las Vegas in December of 1990. The news first appeared in *The Keno Newsletter* (a publication of Shastar Corp, P O Box 19500, Las Vegas, NV 89132). The six-spot ticket cost $3. Six out of six paid $5500, five out of six paid $800, and four out of six paid $15. You can figure out the expected return with the aid of table 13. Your calculations should resemble those of table 14.

Six out of six occurs 0.0129% of the time, or once per 7752 plays. Five out of six occurs 0.310% of the time, or one out of 323 plays. Four out of six occurs 2.85% of the

Table 14
Analysis of Continental's
$3 Six-Spot

spots caught	payoff	probability	product
0	$ 0	.167	$ 0
1	0	.363	0
2	0	.308	0
3	0	.130	0
4	15.00	.0285	0.4275
5	800.00	.00310	2.48
6	5500.00	.000129	0.7095
total			$3.617

time, or once per 35 plays. Multiplying the payoffs times their probabilities and adding them up yields $3.617. So the average $3 wagered returned $3.617, or 120.6%.

Do not rush over to Continental now; the payoff for five out of six has been lowered and you no longer have an edge.

Free $50 Five Spot

One out-of-the-way Las Vegas casino offered anyone a free keno ticket on weekdays. You marked five spots, and if you hit all five you win $50. The ticket was good for every game for five hours.

Table 13 shows the probability of hitting five out of five as 645-003, meaning .000645. Multiplying that by $50 yields an expected value of $0.032 per game. At fourteen or fifteen games per hour, you would win $50 once every 110 hours or so.

Example: Progressive Jackpot

Suppose a casino has a five-spot progressive keno jackpot that starts at $250 and increases by $15 per day. Suppose the ticket costs $1.25. Suppose the payoffs are $30 for catching four spots, and $780 plus the progressive jackpot for catching all five spots. You can figure out how high the jackpot would have to get for you to have an edge over the casino. The calculations are shown in table 15.

The expected return is $0.86 + .000645 times the jackpot. The ticket costs $1.25. Algebra says when the jackpot gets up to about $605 your expectation is to break even, and at jackpots higher than $605 you have an edge.

"What's Hit" Keno

Golden Gate in downtown Las Vegas used to have a board that kept track of how often each ball was drawn.

Table 15
Analysis of Maxim's
Progressive Five-Spot

spots caught	payoff	probability	product
0	$ 0	.227	$0
1	0	.406	0
2	0	.270	0
3	0	.0839	0
4	30	.0121	0.36
5	780+j	.000645	0.50+.000645j
total			$0.86+.000645j

Back in 1979 when I first started writing newsletters, the numbers on the lower half of the board appeared significantly more often than could be due to chance. If you marked enough spots, you had an advantage over the casino on that game. So I know that nonrandom, beatable keno is possible. Do not rush down to Golden Gate to play keno now. The phenomenon disappeared in 1980.

Ever since then I have been wondering about other casinos: Does each keno number really have an equal chance of being selected on each keno game? Unfortunately, casinos that publicize data on keno numbers actually drawn have been rare. So in 1985 I was pleasantly surprised to find that Harvey's Hotel at Stateline had what it called a "what's hit" board in its keno lounge. An advertising flyer says, "If you knew when each Keno number last came up, wouldn't that make you a better player? That's what our new Gold Game frequency board will tell you. And that could be quite an advantage."

I am always looking for an advantage, so I found the "what's hit" board and copied down its numbers. Over the next couple of days I copied down its numbers six more times. At least two hours passed between each of my visits to the keno lounge, so these sets of numbers are independent of each other.

Table 16 contains the numbers I copied down. Each column is a particular observation, and each row is a particular keno ball. The body of the table is games since hit, or GSH. GSH is the number of keno games played since this keno ball last was drawn. A 0 means this ball was drawn on the keno game just finished. A 1 means this ball was drawn on the game before this, and not on this game. A 27 means this ball has not been drawn on any of the last 27 games played.

Table 16
Keno: Games Since Hit
Harvey's Hotel, Stateline

Keno Ball	Observation						
	1	2	3	4	5	6	7
1	1	6	17	5	3	4	0
2	1	3	0	1	2	14	9
3	0	2	0	2	0	19	1
4	3	6	2	3	3	5	2
5	1	0	7	8	1	6	2
6	2	0	11	3	0	0	6
7	2	1	0	5	8	7	6
8	4	1	8	4	6	6	3
9	14	1	0	4	0	5	1
10	0	3	6	1	1	18	12
11	1	3	7	0	2	0	0
12	8	6	1	0	4	9	3
13	1	12	1	7	2	1	6
14	5	2	6	10	0	6	4
15	1	1	8	0	4	0	4
19	1	3	1	3	1	1	0
20	13	1	3	1	0	2	1
21	0	2	4	3	1	0	5
22	2	0	9	7	0	5	8
23	3	2	12	7	6	2	0
24	3	0	3	0	9	2	4
25	8	0	3	0	9	0	0
26	5	0	9	0	4	27	3
27	0	4	0	0	3	7	4
28	4	1	6	1	1	1	5
29	8	4	0	2	3	20	2
30	6	0	0	4	0	4	4
31	1	1	1	3	2	6	1
32	0	5	2	2	4	4	6
33	6	5	3	6	6	0	0
34	6	6	2	3	12	5	3
35	0	9	8	4	1	0	2
36	0	0	0	2	0	9	0
37	0	2	3	0	1	0	2
38	12	0	1	2	0	0	9
39	0	1	7	0	3	1	3
40	2	4	1	9	1	1	1

Table 16 Continued

Keno Ball	Observation						
	1	*2*	*3*	*4*	*5*	*6*	*7*
41	2	2	2	6	1	0	0
42	2	3	7	1	0	1	6
43	0	7	3	0	0	0	16
44	1	0	1	7	2	5	4
45	3	0	6	0	2	0	0
46	1	0	6	8	1	6	4
47	3	0	0	3	3	4	2
48	2	1	0	2	0	12	3
49	0	4	0	8	3	6	2
50	2	1	2	10	1	0	5
51	6	2	0	0	1	0	8
52	2	4	0	2	0	1	0
53	0	2	1	5	3	0	1
54	3	3	0	5	1	2	3
55	2	16	5	2	9	2	2
56	5	7	2	9	5	2	4
57	1	12	4	0	3	2	2
58	0	1	1	0	1	4	5
59	1	0	5	0	0	12	0
60	2	6	1	4	4	1	5
61	0	1	6	0	3	2	0
62	6	2	0	0	2	14	6
63	0	3	12	0	6	0	1
64	6	0	0	1	9	4	1
65	1	0	4	4	2	1	2
66	5	1	5	1	1	0	1
67	1	2	1	4	3	4	3
68	0	0	2	1	2	11	2
69	15	5	1	1	4	0	2
70	0	12	2	0	1	7	9
71	6	4	0	5	2	2	1
72	19	4	10	9	2	1	0
73	0	5	0	3	0	2	12
74	2	3	2	0	0	1	1
75	4	10	1	1	1	2	1
76	10	2	3	2	0	1	0
77	0	1	3	6	0	6	0
78	4	4	2	3	2	11	4
79	1	0	4	5	0	1	0
80	1	3	0	13	4	5	0

Each observation has exactly 20 zeros among the 80 GSH numbers. This is because 20 balls are drawn each game. How often the other numbers occur depends on how much repeating there is from game to game on balls drawn. Some balls are drawn more frequently than others due to chance alone.

If some balls are drawn more frequently than others due to physical differences such as dimensions or weight, then the GSH numbers will be larger than is due to chance alone. They will contain too few small numbers for the balls drawn too often, and too many large numbers for the balls drawn too seldom. So to test Harvey's keno, we compare the actual GSH with what we would have gotten if each ball and each combination of balls has an equal chance of being drawn each game.

For my seven observations, the GSH was slightly but insignificantly greater than the theoretical number. The theoretical average number for GSH is exactly 3, and the variance is 192/7. The average GSH for my seven observations is 3.18. The standard error on the difference between 3 and 3.18 is 0.22 for this sample size, so this difference is not significant.

We are unable to reject the hypothesis that Harvey's keno is completely random. This does not guarantee that this keno game is completely 100% random beyond any doubt whatsoever; there is the possibility of some non-randomness too small to detect with this sample, or nonrandomness of a nature that I have not noticed and have not tested for. But we can say with assurance that if there is any departure from randomness in Harvey's keno, it is too small to be of any value to the players. Therefore, the answer to Harvey's question is no, knowing when each keno number last came up would not make you a better player — at least not at Harvey's keno.

INDEX

ABOUT THE AUTHOR

Stanford Wong is my nom de plume. I was born in 1943. I have a BS and an MBA from Oregon State University, and a Ph.D. in finance from Stanford University. I have taught at several universities, most recently in the 1975-76 school year. I have taught statistics, calculus, linear programming, accounting, and a few finance courses. I have always been an intensely competitive game player, and I like to solve puzzles. I consider myself fortunate that I can spend my time doing things I enjoy doing, and that it pays enough to keep rice on the table.

PUBLICATIONS BY STANFORD WONG

Books

Blackjack

Basic Blackjack is a comprehensive presentation of basic strategy and win rates for all common rules and most exotic rules for the game of blackjack.

Blackjack Secrets is an introduction to card counting (high-low system) and explains how to get away with playing a winning game of blackjack in casinos.

Professional Blackjack is a book with a complete and accurate presentation of the *high-low*, the counting system used by more card counters than any other because of its combination of simplicity and power. If you want a more advanced counting system, *Professional Blackjack* also contains the *halves*.

Casino Tournaments

Casino Tournament Strategy is the book that explains how to get an edge over the other players in tournaments. It covers blackjack, craps, baccarat, and keno.

The strategies required for success in a blackjack tournament are completely different from the strategies that a professional blackjack player would use to support himself.

A skillful tournament player has a bigger edge in a crap tournament than in a blackjack tournament. This is due to two things: there is a multitude of possible bets, and all contestants bet on the same rolls of the dice.

In April 1990 Anthony Curtis won the $125,000 first prize in a crap tournament at Atlantic City. Curtis helped develop the material in *Casino Tournament Strategy*.

Video Poker

Professional Video Poker is the book that shows how to get an edge on video poker at both Nevada and Atlantic City casinos. The material was developed with the aid of two video-poker pros. (Yes, there are people who support themselves playing video poker.)

Pai Gow Poker

Optimal Strategy For Pai Gow Poker is the book that shows how to get an edge at pai gow poker. Jeff Mervis, who helped create the material in this book, supports himself by playing pai gow poker in the card casinos of California. Mike Caro, author of *Professional Pai Gow Poker Report*, says "Those serious players seeking to make a living at pai gow poker will find Wong's *Optimal Strategy for Pai Gow Poker* an almost perfect path to profit." New in the 1992 edition: a chapter on pai gow poker tournaments.

Betting on Horses

If you are intrigued by the possibility of betting on horses and want to learn something about it, *Betting Cheap Claimers* is a good place to start. It explains how to get a big edge in handicapping tournaments. It explains two methods a casual casino racebook customer can use to find bets with a positive expectation, and backs up both with empirical tests that have statistical significance. It discusses money management. It also has an introduction to handicapping, a glossary, and an index.

Newsletter

Current Blackjack News, a newsletter for blackjack players, has been published monthly since 1979, and monthly plus special editions since 1992. It has had some spectacular news items. April 1993: Saddle West in Pahrump adds a joker to each shoe; your edge with basic strategy is 2.1% or more. April 1993: Las Vegas Hilton allows you to make another bet and receive another hand if you stand on your first hand; your edge with basic strategy is 1.9%. December 1992: Nevada Hotel in Las Vegas gives a coupon book to hotel guests; one coupon can be used as an ace as your first card at blackjack, for a bet of up to $200. September 1992: Continental in Las Vegas pays a $100 bonus for two consecutive naturals. September 1991: Maxim deals 51 of the 52 cards at single deck, with good rules. August 1991: Frontier deals single deck with rules so liberal that basic strategy gives you a 0.3% edge. January 1990: Sahara deals baccarat without a commission; flat $100 bets on the bank have the expectation of winning $1000 per evening. November 1989: Marina issues a coupon book worth about $1000; you can use one per day. October 1989: Sands deals blackjack with three jokers per six-deck shoe. *Current Blackjack News* is available by fax as well as by mail.

Software

Blackjack Count Analyzer is a computer program for playing blackjack. It works on IBM PCs and compatible computers. Besides playing blackjack, *Blackjack Count Analyzer* generates tables of strategy indexes and runs high-speed simulations. It handles all common and uncommon rules variations, and also some rules variations that have never been offered in any casino.

An earlier version of it, *Blackjack Analyzer*, is available also; *Blackjack Analyzer* uses basic strategy only, whereas *Blackjack Count Analyzer* supports card counting.

Stanford Wong Video Poker, like its predecessor *Video Poker Analyzer,* is a computer program for playing and analyzing video poker. *VPEXACT* cycles through all possible video poker hands and finds the payback percentage—for any pay schedule. These programs work on IBM PCs and compatible computers.

Speedy Hold 'Em is a computer program for playing hold 'em, a poker game. It also works on IBM PCs and compatible computers.

Ordering Information

Write to Pi Yee Press, 7910 Ivanhoe #34, La Jolla, CA 92037-4511 for prices and an order form. Or call (619) 456-4080.